CREATIVITY MATTERS

FIND YOUR PASSION FOR WRITING

WENDY H. JONES

Tracy
all the best with
your own writing
Wendy H. Jones

SCOTT AND LAWSON

www.wendyhjones.com

Cover design by Cathy Helms of Avalon Graphics LLC

ISBN: 978-1-913372-03-3

For all those who have been a part of my writing journey. I am eternally grateful for your support.

To all the authors who have contributed to this book, it is all the better for your input. May your words continue to flow and your ideas continue to grow. Know you are amazing.

CONTENTS

HOW TO USE THIS BOOK

Welcome to *Creativity Matters*. Like all the books in the *Writing Matters* series it is designed to be used in multiple ways and to suit all writing styles and approaches.

You may want to read it t cover to cover enjoying the chapters and absorbing them as you go through. I can assure you this will be an enjoyable experience and will have your creative brain blowing up as you do so. Ideas will be popping up and exploding all around you. This is your chance to harness this increased creativity.

You may want to start with the chapters which most resonate with you and focus on those to start with. This is equally valid and an individual choice. Be sure you return to the other chapters as you may miss out on an experience which will transform your writing journey.

Whichever way you approach the book, I would advise you to do so with a notebook and pen to hand. As ideas come to you jot them down. If something resonates with you take notes. If your reading sparks an idea which could lift your current work in progress and make it pop from the page then don't lose it. The book is there to be used and you should use it widely and wisely. This book, your brain, and your notebook are a powerful combination which will revolutionise your creative process.

My last piece of advice - enjoy the journey.

INTRODUCTION

Whether you are thinking of becoming a writer, are new to the writing journey or are an experienced writer this book is for you. I would like to start by asking two questions? Why do I think creativity matters and why should you read a book about it? Before answering these let's be honest and say this book deals with creative passion for writing as the subtitle suggests. Although, as will become clear throughout the book, other creative endeavours also feed into the writing process. Writing can, and indeed should, involve all our senses and utilise both sides of our brain. But, for the purposes of clarity, let's focus on writing.

Creative writing – I will be bold here and say all writing involves some degree of creativity – performs essential functions in our lives. It helps us develop our communication and thinking skills as we look at how words work and how they can be manipulated to enhance, clarify or change meaning. Learning new words and working out how they can be used is something which comes naturally, and we are programmed to do so. Think of a child's joy as they learn a new word and use it correctly; the writer feels similar joy when using words to create their manuscript. Writing also allows us to express who we are and demonstrate our individuality. We are all unique and this uniqueness will come through in the writing process, demonstrated by the different stories which are written within a group given the same writing prompt. No two will be the same and even if there are similar themes, the way they are written, and the twists used will be unique. Creative writing also allows us to bring joy to others who read our works. Consider this:

> 'I read a book one day and my whole life was changed.'
> Orhan Pamuk

Although this is from a novel, I think Panuk has, in this line, encapsulated why most writers write. What you write can change people's lives. There is no greater feeling than when readers say they enjoy your books and can't wait for the next one to come out. Knowing that you are somehow making someone's life better is both an honour and a privilege.

So, why should you read this book? I believe it will open you up to new ideas and new ways of thinking. If a new writer, it will introduce you to the possibilities that lie before you and the exciting journey you are facing. If an established writer, it will introduce you to new possibilities and may lead to exhilarating new paths for you to explore. Welcome to a whole new world of creativity and I am sure you will enjoy taking the journey through the chapters with the authors as your guides as they share their passion for writing.

1

WHY WRITE?

WENDY H. JONES

Where does one start when writing a book on creativity which focuses on finding your passion for writing or, indeed your passion for writing in different genres if already an established writer. One feels there should be a stirring refrain: a quote from a notable writer: a cry from the heart: a passionate speech or at the very least something which tantalises and intrigues. The fact of the matter is, all these things will be covered throughout the chapter as I introduce you to why I am passionate about writing, and why I feel this is a passion which everyone, including you, can discover, develop, and cherish. Each chapter in the book covers a different genre with authors who have a deep and abiding passion for writing within that genre. Indeed, I, too, have written chapters sharing my passion. However, I wanted to start by looking at why we write at all.

At a basic level, we write to communicate because there is something we want to share. As a writing coach and tutor, I often hear the refrain, "I can't write." Let me unpack that.

Unless you are physically unable to write because you have not yet learned to do so, then everyone can write. I would bet my granny on the fact those uttering the phrase write emails, letters, documents, social media posts etc. almost every day. What they mean is, I don't yet know how to *write* a story of any kind. There are two important words in this sentence. The first is yet and the second is write. I have deliberately italicised the word write, and I will come onto this in a moment. First, I would like to open discussion about the word yet. I believe that everyone has the potential to learn how to write stories. Why do I believe that? It's simple; if you ask anyone to tell you a story about their life, they will wax lyrical and *tell* you that story. Everyone has the ability to tell stories, they just need encouragement to produce those stories in written form.

Stories have been told throughout history, both through oral tradition and in cave paintings. The first evidence of painted stories dates from over 30,000 years ago and was discovered in Lascaux and Chavaux in France. According to the British Library the first written characters, and thus the earliest form of writing, appeared about 5,500 years ago. The oldest surviving literary work is thought to be Homer's *The Iliad* in the crossover from oral to written tradition. So, we are all genetically programmed to be storytellers and it would appear to be fear of the written word that puts would be writers off. "That's all very well," I hear you say, "but what does this have to do with me? I've been writing for years." You raise a fair point, yet I would like to venture that you have settled into a certain groove, writing the same things you have always written. When was the last time you tried something new? When was the last time you stepped out of your comfort zone? At the thought of this are you feeling a faint stirring of fear, the same fear you felt when you first started writing? It is harnessing that fear and channelling it into words that makes us write or makes us fly as a writer when trying new things.

Whilst we all write to communicate every day, this does not bear a passion inside us. It's something we have to do, and I think this is where many would-be writers flounder. They may have struggled at school or do not enjoy the formal aspects of writing and view it as a necessary evil. They may have been told they cannot write or that writing is not a real job. They may have an idea for a story or a book, but they just do not feel they have the skills to get it down on paper. Established writers may have been told, stick to what you know. Does any of this resonate with you?

Story drives passion and when it comes to writing, passion is everything. This is not a how to book, so I will not be telling you how to get started but having a story inside you bursting to get out is half the battle. It's a feeling like no other where it bubbles and bubbles away deep inside until it boils over, and the words spill on to the page. I know I write because I can't not write. Writing is as natural as breathing to me. I have been writing stories as long as I can remember, and I love story-telling.

'If there's a book that you want to read, but it hasn't been written yet, then you must write it.'
Toni Morrison

Nearly every great writer is first a great reader. Reading stimulates our brains and allows us to develop and grow in our use of language. I would like to ask you a question – do you read? I know the answers will fall into four camps.

1. I love reading and am never without a book.
2. Occasionally
3. I used to but I don't have time anymore.
4. No. I hate reading.

If you are a passionate reader, I applaud you. If you read occasionally, I would encourage you to read more often. If you feel that number three fits your lifestyle, then may I ask you to do one thing? Look at your phone or tablet and in settings check out the amount of time you spend online per day. I can almost guarantee you will be shocked. If your result said 'last week you averaged 3.5 hours per day online' you will be saying, I didn't spend that much time on my phone/tablet. If you love reading but have fallen out of the habit due to time, it may be useful to think about how you use your time. Not only will you rediscover your enjoyment of reading, but your eyes will thank you. If you fall into the fourth camp then again, I will challenge you. Do you read newspapers? Social media posts? Online articles about things that interest you? If the answer to this is yes, then I would encourage you to visit your local library, discuss your interests with the librarian and he or she will help you to find a book that you might enjoy. Why am I talking about reading in a chapter about writing? The answer is simple – I would strongly encourage you to not only read but read widely. Read magazines, newspapers, short stories, flash fiction, novels, articles, non-fiction, and do so in different genres. Developing a habit of reading will allow you to be more creative and help you in developing a habit of writing. It will allow you to expand your vocabulary and to see how good writing is done. Fill your brain with words in all their richness. Find your passion for reading and your brain, luxuriating in the words your read, will have your mind filled to overflowing with stories just waiting to be written. Reading and writing are inextricably linked.

Reading great books will inspire you to emulate the greatest writers and give you the powers and the process by which it can be done. We write because we are inspired and because we have a love affair with words.

'I believe that reading and writing are the most nourishing forms of meditation anyone has so far found. By reading the writings of the most interesting minds in history, we meditate with our own minds and theirs as well. This to me is a miracle.'

Kurt Vonnegut

I will assume as you are reading this book you want, as the subtitle suggests, to develop your passion for writing. Yet, you may be thinking, as many others do, I do not want to share my writing with anyone. That is absolutely fine. When it comes to writing we either do it for ourselves or for others. Writing a journal or diary is equally as satisfying as writing the next Booker Prize winning novel. All writing is equally valid, and you choose what to do with the finished product. You may want to write a novel to prove to yourself you can do it. If that is your choice, then have at it. Writing should, and will, allow for personal fulfilment. All writing is personal whether it is done for publication, for future family generations to read, or for your own enjoyment.

Often, we start writing because there is a topic about which we are passionate and/or are knowledgeable. Does this describe you? Then consider a book based on this passion. When people say to me, they want to write a book but don't know what to write about, I start by putting this aside and then spend ten minutes chatting to them about themselves, their interests, and their hobbies. By the end of this conversation, it is usually clear they have a passion that would make a fabulous book. When I reflect this back to them their eyes light up. Usually, the block to starting to write is that nearly every person who wants to write a book starts with the premise they should write a novel. The truth is all writers should write what they are comfortable writing and what they enjoy writing. Think about what you enjoy doing or enjoy talking about – does this lend itself to a non-fiction book or even a fictionalised version of a true story. You may believe that no one would find your story interesting as it is a niche market. Visit any bookshop and you will find books written for those who are interested in niche topics. I can assure you if you find a topic interesting then so will others, so do not dismiss the power of the passion you have for a topic.

When talking about discovering your passion for writing you should not ignore the fact that whilst writing you are also learning. Writers, no matter the stage of their journey, are constantly learning; every day brings a new challenge and a new discovery. I can almost hear you say, "What? Learning? Challenges? That sounds like hard work." Yes, writing can be hard work, but at the same time is also worthwhile and enjoyable. The challenge is to grow and develop and along the way become a better writer. Learning comes as you research different aspects of your story or non-fiction narrative. All forms of writing require research – even fiction. For example, I write a police procedural series, *The DI Shona McKenzie Mysteries*. This involves me researching different aspects of policing in Scotland. At one point, I had my main characters going to a lap dancing club; trust me, I know nothing about lap dancing. During the research process I learned many interesting facts, a great deal of which will never make it into my books. However, the facts are stored in my brain and in notebooks and you never know when they will become useful. Here's an example. Did you know the last person hanged for fraud in the UK was a banker? He pleaded guilty and said he did it for the good of the bank. He was hanged anyway as they said his defence was weak. Whilst you will not read about this in any book except this one, I have used it during a book signing in a bank. Yes, I really did a book signing tour of Scottish banks. This fascinating fact was a way of chatting to people and helping them become aware of my books. Not only does research help my writing but it also helps me to be a well-rounded person with a wealth of knowledge.

I believe writing to be the best job in the world because the writer, through their works brings enjoyment to those who read them. It is an honour and a privilege to know that someone has bought a book with my name on the front and has enjoyed reading it. Let this writer tell you there is no better feeling. When readers say they can't wait for your next book to come out, it is thrilling. This drives the writer's passion and is what keeps them writing. Seeing your books on the shelves in bookshops, whether physical or virtual, is equally as thrilling.

As a writer I feel like I am a part of literary history. Knowing that I am joining the ranks of a long heritage of Scottish writers fills me with awe – writers such as Sir Walter Scott, Sir Arthur Conan Doyle, Robert Louis Stephenson, Muriel Spark, JM Barrie, need I go on? The lineage of great Scottish Writers throughout the centuries is long and contains far too many names to mention in one short chapter. I appreciate not everyone reading this book is from Scotland but researching great writers in your own country will be equally awe inspiring; I can guarantee it. When I write I feel like I am a part of something so much greater than me.

Writing makes us more observant as we study everyone and everything around us. We take in sights, sounds and smells, internalise them and use them in our writing. It is this intent observation which provides richness to our writing and makes us better writers. It also makes us curious as we wonder why a particular event happened and the effect it had on all those associated with it or the effect on the wider world. Again, this questioning makes us better writers as it gives depth and meaning to what we write. The same holds true whether writing fiction or non-fiction. Every great writer starts by being curious.

It has been suggested that writing gives us a meaning and a sense of our place in the world. I would agree with this but would add it is also fun. Writing gives free range to our imagination and gives our brain permission to go places that real life would not allow. For established writers, writing in different genres gives a similar sense of freedom. It encourages the writer to use a different type of creativity and sets their imagination free.

As you have read this, I hope my words have ignited your own passion for writing and/or taking your writing in a new direction. I will finish with the words of iconic writer, Umberto Eco.

'To survive, you must tell stories.'

Telling stories is the most miraculous, liberating, exciting, freeing, feeling in the world. This is why I write and why I would encourage you to do so also. Read the remainder of this book and find your own passion for writing amongst the different genres that are covered. You won't regret it.

Author Bio

Wendy H. Jones is an award-winning, international best-selling author of fifteen books in five different series, covering readers from childhood to adulthood. These include adult crime, young adult mysteries, children's picture books, and non-fiction for writers. She is currently writing a historical fiction book, the first in a new series. In addition, she is a writing coach, editor, and CEO of *Authorpreneur Accelerator Academy* - a membership supporting authors on their writing and publishing journey - and runs S*cott and Lawson Publishing*. You can find out more at http://www.wendyhjones.com

2

WHY WRITE HISTORIC NON-FICTION?

SHEENA MACLEOD

Have you ever come across something from the past and found yourself saying, 'I want to write about that?' Chances are, there is a story there trying to get out. For many, this will be in the form of historical non-fiction, rather than historical fiction. This might involve a desire to write a factual account of historical events experienced by a stranger or family member, or something from your own life.

My desire to write historical non-fiction came late in life. After years of academic writing as a lecturer in mental health nursing, I found that my passion for research had also led me in the direction of researching history in an attempt to better understand my heritage. In 2009, I was diagnosed with Lupus, an auto-immune disorder, and decided to retire. Building up to this, I had developed a desire to write about the history I had been researching and reading about but pushed the idea away as something I would never actually do. No one was more surprised than me when I decided to do just that. Retirement had afforded me the time to write the stories I wanted to tell.

Although I enjoy reading a wide range of genres, I prefer fact-based historical fiction and non-fiction, so it seemed natural for me to move in this direction once I started writing. Before long, I had moved my research from reading about my period of interest and visiting historical sites and buildings, to researching the people who lived then and trying to understand what life was like for them as they lived through the events I had been reading about. I wondered how people managed to survive, or not, some of the dark times of the past. I began to realise and admire the resilience and courage of some, and watched great leaders emerge who fought back against the injustices of many. I regarded them all as people of courage.

When it comes to history, like many, I am drawn to certain time periods. With so many thousands of years behind us, it is unsurprising to have a passion for one era, rather than another. It is also not unusual to develop knowledge about a particular place. For me, that place is Scotland, in particular the Scottish Highlands. I lived for many years in the Scottish Borders, and my father grew up in Stornoway on the Isle of Lewis, where some of my relatives still live. In terms of time period, my interest lies in the 17th – 19th century. Regardless of location and time period, I am drawn towards strong women in history.

It was with some sadness as I grew older that I came to the realisation that I had huge gaps in my understanding of the history of my country. Like many others who grew up in and experienced the Scottish education system of the '60s, the history I was taught at school consisted largely of rote learning of key events - mainly battles, along with dates and key figures. And, the focus was on England, with little, if anything, included about Scotland.

Fortunately, I also grew up on a diet of books in which I could select the era and place of interest I chose to read about. The past is indeed a foreign country and I just loved visiting these places in my mind's eye. Growing up in the Scottish Borders, I stayed very near to the home of Walter Scott, one of the greatest Scottish writers of his time. The area is also steeped in history. From tales of the Anglo-Scottish Border Reivers, in the 14th -17th century, when Scots raided the English to plunder and steal cattle and vice versa, and experiencing the traditional annual Common Ridings, where some Scottish Border towns commemorated this with people riding around their boundaries on horseback – Riding of the Marches – re-enacting and keeping alive their role in defending Scotland from English invaders, to the majestic Eildon Hill with its remnants of an old Roman Fort, plus a wealth of old abbeys such as Melrose and Kelso Abbey, I felt is if I was growing up on the edge of history. The present and the past merging as one.

My desire to write historical non-fiction came from what I perceived as a lack of information about the history of the clearances carried out in Scotland during the 18th and 19th century, particularly in the Highlands and Islands. My father grew up in a crofting community. When I visited my grandparents there, I could see how hard crofting life was and heard stories and imagined that it must have been even harder in times past. But, unlike my experience of the history of the Borders, where this was made open to the public and celebrated, the history of the Highlands and Islands felt silent, as if it hadn't happened at all and it was certainly not something you talked about then. While this has now changed, and is continuing to change, it was as if there was an embarrassment then about the history of these places, and I wanted to find out more.

Some areas of history have been widely written about, such as the Tudor period, both in historical fiction and historical non-fiction, but there are many lesser-known areas, like the Scottish Clearances, hidden or ignored with little written about them. There is also much forgotten history – of events or experiences which have been written out or written over, or a one-sided view presented. These 'missing' histories are the areas I am most drawn to. Like a giant jigsaw puzzle with only the edges in place, I feel the need to fill in the blanks that would make up the picture inside. My interest is thus piqued, and the research begins.

The extent of research involved in writing historical non-fiction is not for the faint-hearted and requires a high level of dedication and determination to see it through. It also requires access to resources. This can involve a great deal of time and sometimes support from others, such as librarians or archivists, to access texts and documents required. While this can be frustrating when searches lead to dead ends, it can also be highly rewarding when nuggets of new information are unearthed. Up until the 20th century, history was mostly written by men, as they were more in a position to do so than women who may not have had the same opportunity. As a result, much early history is based around a man's view of battles fought and wars won or lost and the politics and intrigues of the time. What I am usually looking for, however, is the women's perspective. How did women manage when men were away at war? What contribution did women make, why and how?

Although it is no substitute for visiting places, the internet opens up a whole new world of information and resources to historical writers that was never available before. I love visiting museums and historical buildings to see artefacts of the time, but also enjoy the ability to look at these online where I can examine them in more detail and read what others have said about them. I also wanted to focus on how people lived at the time - what they believed and the events they encountered as they went about their everyday life.

During the '70s and '80s, while working as a nurse in various psychiatric hospitals, prior to the introduction of community care mental health policies, I developed an interest in the patients' experiences of living in these institutions. Nellie Bly's, *Ten Days in a Madhouse* provides a fascinating, if shocking, true

account of the ten days American investigative journalist Elizabeth Cochrane Seaman (aka Nellie Bly) spent in an insane
asylum in New York City in 1887. A few years before this,
Charles Dickens had visited this asylum and wrote a harrowing
account of the dreadful conditions he saw there. While Dickens
had visited the asylum, Nellie Bly had lived it and then
reported her findings. In doing so, they both opened up this
hidden world to public view.

Another book that had a huge influence on me during this
time was Barbara Robb's exposé published in 1967 of the inhu-
mane treatment of the elderly in long stay psychiatric hospital
wards in in the UK. In *Sans Everything: A Case to Answer*, Robb
exposed over-crowding, under-staffing and rough nursing prac-
tices towards the elderly residents and rushed 'production-line'
care with little or no medical treatments or attempts at rehabili-
tation. This was a pivotal book for the redesign and improve-
ment of geriatric services in the UK. It also further drew my
awareness to hidden histories. Robb was a psychotherapist and
campaigner for change. Without her exposé it is doubtful if the
voices of the elderly in geriatric hospital wards would have
been heard or reported at this time.

Novels which helped develop my passion for Scottish
history and a desire to know more include those by Neil Gunn,
in particular, *Silver Darlings*, 1941, which depicts the hard life
and resilience of people forced from their homes in the inner
straths in the North of Scotland to work on the fisheries on the
coast. Unlike Gunn's novels, much historical fiction presents a
romanticised view of life in the Scottish Highlands at this time.
The same was evident in much of the fictional literature based
around Charkes II's Court in London during the 17th century.
This was the spur for me to present a realistic, rather than
romanticised view of these eras in my own writing.

My first foray into historical writing was a fact-based historical novel set in Restoration London, *Reign of the Marionettes'*

published in 2017. While this might seem surprising, given that my area of interest lay at a later time in Scotland, I soon realised through my research that the only way for me to understand and write about this time was to look at what had happened in Restoration London and then follow the ripple effect of this back to Scotland. Much of what was written at this time was about England, and in a way that ignored the impact on Scotland. And it did have an impact. Most of the historical events that arose later in Scotland derived from what happened around this time in England.

Historical writing can be time consuming, but it's worth it to see the end results. While there are overlaps between historical fiction and historical non-fiction writing in the search for historical accuracy there are major differences too. When writing fact-based historical fiction gaps in knowledge can be filled in while the non-fiction writer has to dig deeper and if nothing emerges then these gaps have to be acknowledged as just that, gaps for further study.

Historical non-fiction writing also involves more than presenting the facts. It also requires these facts to be analysed. Historical events didn't just happen in a vacuum and they need to be understood in relation to the wider context and world stage. Newspapers and pamphlets are available from the time periods I was interested in. The broadsheets of 17th century London were written so that they were accessible to the common - mostly illiterate - people of the time, through pictures, and ballads that would be sung in taverns and in the street until even the children had learned them. Much 'false news' was spread this way and was often designed to instil fear and obedience in the common people. Hangings were public events, and the day was announced as a holiday to enable people to attend so that they could witness for themselves the end result of breaking the law. After the hanging, the last dying statements of the deceased were distributed to the public. Readers now are not just interested in the events that happened but also why they happened, and this is where my own area of interest lies.

In the book I am in the process of completing, *Tears of Strathnaver,* a fact-based historical novel set at the turn of the 19th century in the north of Scotland, I was able to draw on an archaeological dig that had been carried out and had uncovered long houses used by tenant farmers in the area at that time. It also showed the layout of the houses and outbuildings within this small-farming community prior to it being cleared of tenants. I was also fortunate to have access to a detailed documented account written at the time by a minister of the Parish as well as access to the Military Register newspaper which reported on these events at the time from the perspective of the tenant farmers. The tenants themselves left few formal documented accounts of their experience, while there were copious notes and tracts written by the landlord and their commissioners offering their own accounts. The poetry of the time is revealing, and details from the report of the Napier Commission into the public enquiry carried out later in 1884, of the condition of cottars and crofters in the Highlands and Islands of Scotland, provided further information.

My dive into writing historical non-fiction, rather than dramatising actual events, happened by chance. A global group of writers, artists and musicians came together to raise money and awareness for Cancer Research UK and the homeless through the charity EMMAUS under the banner of the One Million Project (OMP). In 2017, The founder, Jason Greenfield, came across an article written by Laura Linham, a reporter with the newspaper, *Somerset Live,* about a report published in 1911 about Frances Connelly, a working-class woman who voted before the time it was legal for women to do so in the UK. As the 100-year celebration of women gaining the legal right to vote in parliamentary elections was coming up the following year, I was commissioned to research and write a book about Frances Connelly. I contacted Laura Linham, as little was known or written about Frances Connelly, and she agreed to co-author a book with me on Frances and how this woman had managed to vote in a by-election and raise the question in some people's minds 'If one woman could vote why not all?' We also decided to look at the wider role played by working-class women in the women's suffragist movement. The book, *So, You Say I Can't Vote. Frances Connelly: The working-class woman's route to the vote*, was published in 2018 with all proceeds going to the OMP.

We live in a world with a growing fascination with the past. Exposure to history is now an everyday occurrence for most. As people's access to history, through news, documentary reports, films and historical books has increased, so too has people's knowledge and readiness to engage with and challenge many traditionally held views, and to write about this through historical non-fiction books, articles and even blogs. As a result, much history is now being rewritten and added to by non-historians. While there is much that can't be verified, historical knowledge is increasing all the time and it is rewarding to be able to add to this store, even if it is in the smallest of ways.

Memoirs have become highly popular with readers, myself included, and it's not just famous historical events or figures people are interested in. Memoirs can provide 'a slice of life' from any time period. In *The Grocer's Boy* and *The Grocer's Boy Rides Again*, Scottish author Robert Murray recounts his memories of growing up in the East of Scotland and working in the grocery trade during the 1950s and 1960s; in doing so he preserves the history and the culture of this time.

For me, writing historical fiction and non-fiction came from a need to understand more about my country and cultural heritage. I am interested in how cultural identity is constructed over time and the marginalisation of particular subgroups within this. Exposure to divergent accounts of the past forced me to rethink the history I had been taught at school and find new ways of looking at this. Fortunately, as an avid reader, I soon came to realise that what I was reading, beyond the history books, through social and cultural histories, biographies, memoirs, and historical fiction based on realistic rather than romanticised views of the time had already made me start to question what I had been taught and seek out alternative narratives.

Having been through the process a few times since my initial foray into writing historical non-fiction, I have no shortage of ideas for further books and articles. While the research involved was time consuming, it was also immensely enjoyable, particularly when digging a little deeper uncovered some gems. Is writing historical non-fiction hard work? Yes, it can be. Is it worth it? Absolutely.

Author Bio

Sheena Macleod lives in a seaside town in Scotland. She gained a PhD at the University of Dundee, where she lectured in mental health nursing. She has a number of published short stories and articles. *Reign of the Marionettes* is her first published historical fiction novel. *So, You Say I Can't Vote! Frances Connelly: The Working-class Woman's Route to the Vote*, a non-fiction book, was co-written with journalist, Laura Linham.

https://www.sheenas-books.co.uk

WHY WRITE CHILDREN'S BOOKS?

JANET WILSON

A few years ago, I planned to visit an Asian country, for which I needed a visa. My son was living there, and I was looking forward to staying with him and meeting his wife-to-be.

When I arrived at the visa application office in London, a row of booths was buzzing with would-be travellers, handing in their papers to official-looking people in smart suits. When it came to my turn, the official went over my application methodically, line by line. When it came to my job description, he raised his eyebrows and asked me what I published. "Children's books," I told him, with a smile. I thought that ought to be safe. What could be more innocuous than children's books? The official didn't smile back.

Further down the form, my place of work was listed: *Dernier Publishing.*

He typed something into his computer and frowned. "These are religious books," the man said.

I nodded. "Christian fiction," I replied. The country in question allows freedom of religion, on paper at least, so I didn't think there should be a problem.

The official carried on typing and scrolling. After a while, he requested my mobile phone number. I hesitated. If I gave it, it meant his government could keep tabs on me, but if I didn't give it, I might not get the visa...

I gave it.

Have a nice day, I was hearing, as people in other cubicles who had arrived after me were leaving, papers in hand.

"Wait here please," my official said. He left his cubicle and went out the back.

My heart was beating fast by the time he returned, with a pen and a sheet of paper. He passed both under the safety glass to me. I had to write with my own hand, then sign and date a declaration, in which I promised that I would not take part in any publishing or media activities during my stay in that country.

I got my visa, but the whole experience made a deep impression on me.

What our children read is way, way more important than we realise. What our children put in their minds when they are young, will affect the whole of their lives.

Here in the West, we tend to think about children's books as harmless fun, but dictators, communists, despots... *they know the effect books can have on children.*

We ought to sit up and take notice.

Malala Yousafzai was shot by the Taliban in 2012, when she was a 14-year-old student. Her dad wanted her to have an education, but the Taliban didn't. Why wouldn't anyone want their girls to be educated? Because they don't want them to think.

Adolf Hitler knew this, too. In his book *Mein Kampf,* he said, "Whoever has the youth has the future." Every child had to study *Mein Kampf* at school, while books opposing the Nazi regime were banned and burned.

What power there is in a book! Words can enslave, or they can set free.

Writing children's books is an awesome responsibility.

If you are reading this, I'm going to assume that you are of the opinion that children should have access to all kinds of books and reading material (within reason), so they can make up their own minds about life and all its issues. At Dernier Publishing we think all children should have access to Christian books, *not to convert them*, but so they can decide for themselves.

Books open up possibilities. Would you like to open up possibilities for children, through your words? To show them how things work in this crazy world, and how to make it a better place? To show them that their life matters, that the choices they make affect their lives, that they are beautiful and infinitely precious? If you do, perhaps writing for children is for you.

Mostly, when we think of children's books, we think of stories. Who doesn't love a good story, with engaging characters and a gripping plot? Ever since man sat round a campfire thousands of years ago, we have been telling each other stories. In a way, we make sense of our world through story – story is a powerful tool, as well as being a lot of fun. We can learn so much through a good book!

Do you have a treasured, dog-eared book or two from childhood? I still have my old copy of *Little House on the Prairie* (with the price stamped on the back: 25p)! Just the smell of the book takes me back to the days when I read on the stairs if there wasn't anywhere else to go. I read it purely for enjoyment, but it taught me about families and simple pleasures, about loyalty and pulling together, about hardship and celebrations, about faith, struggles and community.

When my children were growing up, story time was one of the favourite times of the day. Sometimes we'd get so lost in a story that my children would beg me for one more chapter, *pleeeaaase!* What joy there was in curling up with a good book together and being whisked off to far-off places and adventures in time and space. Other times we'd read about the moon, or tigers, or pyramids. All were precious times of learning, of closeness, of shared experience and relationships grown.

None of these times would have been possible without authors – people like you and me, who put pen to paper, or fingers to keyboard.

Small children need picture books with stories which teach them about the world in which they live. Older children need adventure stories with characters like themselves, who solve crimes, save their family, find the treasure, deal with bullies, train the dragons, destroy the evil empire, make it to safety after their city is bombed... They need stories to enjoy that will bring light and life and hope – stories that can give a sense of perhaps I could do that, too. In one of our Dernier books (*Deepest Darkness*), Abi lives her life full of fear. By the end of the story, she has found a chink of light in her darkness. Many readers have found that they, too, can find hope, just as Abi did. In *Revenge of the Flying Carpet*, Paul seeks revenge on his sister, but things don't work out the way he thinks they should. My latest novel, *Year 0033* is set in the future when religion is banned. It's worth thinking about these things. Why not through a story?

If this possibility excites you, perhaps you could write for children.

But you don't have to write fiction!

You could write how-to books on creepy crawlies, cookery, or collecting coins. You could write inspiring biographies, or maths books that make learning fun! You could write about parakeets, continental shift, or costumes from different countries.

Writing isn't just for books, either. You could write screenplays, theatre plays, sketches for schools, prayers, or internet articles.

All you need to do is to match up your interest with the

needs of your potential readers, and you're good to go! There's so much opportunity!

Excited? I am. And there's more...

I received a letter from a teacher recently. Schools are desperate for books that deal with mental health issues, including anxiety surrounding identity, loss, anorexia, suicidal tendencies, bereavement, body dysmorphia and self-harm. Children need story books that demonstrate empathy, and there's a lack of books with girls as strong characters... could you help? Have you been through any of these struggles? Could you write a book that would help someone else to survive and thrive?

Books help readers feel understood. The feeling that we are not alone is a very precious thing. If you had a difficult childhood, perhaps you could share your experiences in a novel. The stories we resonate with most, are the stories we can see ourselves in.

Books change lives – teachers know it – we all know it. Even one book can have a knock-on effect. A single sunflower seed, when planted, can bear hundreds of seeds! Readers make leaders. You never know what influence your book might have.

I have a friend who grew up in a Christian home. Every year she was given a book from the Sunday School. She treasured these books as she grew in her own faith. Years later, she lent one of these books to her own daughter who was going through a traumatic time. It was a turning point in her life.

Words are powerful. Books can give a child a sense of purpose, lift them out of their circumstances, warn them of danger, give them something to aim for.

Books are also, at their most fundamental, part of life's education. Books can literally help to lift a child out of poverty. I don't need to tell you that if you can't read, you are unlikely to go far in life. Sadly, prisoners are disproportionately illiterate in comparison with the rest of the population.

There are 1.9 billion children in the world – every one is precious, and should have the opportunity of an education, so they can learn and grow and love and give. Dernier sends boxes of books to Education Bridge Africa, an organisation in Uganda that takes books to desperately poor schools. Dr Loise Gichuhi, from the organisation, told me that some slum schools have *no reading books* – imagine that! These books are bringing life and hope.

Book poverty isn't just for Africa, either. A 2019 survey in the UK by the National Literacy Trust showed that 383,775 children do not own a book. Not a single book!

For a rounded education, children need books that are relevant, fun and inspirational.

That starts with authors like you and me.

If you were an avid reader as a child; could you now inspire a whole new generation of children with your own books?

If at this point part of you is saying, "Yes, I'd love to do that," but the other part of you is objecting, "Are you kidding?"...don't worry. You can start small.

If you and your daughter have a joint interest in butterflies, why not write a book for her... and get her to illustrate it? Or how about writing your first ever story for a nephew, where he and his pets go through all kinds of adventures before defeating... well, I'll leave that up to you!

Your first story doesn't have to be a printed book. You could record yourself reading it or post it on your Facebook page. You could print it out and put it in a folder or have it spiral-bound. You could make it into an ebook/kindle book for no cost (your reader might even be able to help you do that!).

There's nothing wrong with a small start.

You don't know how far your book could go, though. A story on kindle could be read by a family in Nepal, or by an abused child in an inner city. Your prayer posted online could touch a child in a Brazilian slum or in a millionaire's mansion in Los Angeles.

There's no doubt about it, writing for children is an awesome responsibility and an enormous privilege. If you don't feel up to the challenge, no worries, buy books for them instead! But if you are feeling a stirring in your heart, and you would like to leave a legacy with your words, remember this: you are unique. No one else is like you. No one else has your experiences, your gifts, your take on life. If you don't write your book, no one else can write it for you. Don't ignore the call.

I teach creative writing to writers who are new to writing fiction for children. The material has a Christian slant, because I am a Christian, but almost all the material is equally relevant, whatever you believe. We discuss characters, themes, plots, settings, narrative voice and so much more. If you come on over to write-for-a-reason.com, I'd love to be able to help you take the next step in your writing journey.

AuthorBio

Following her first husband's death in 2003, Janet Wilson began writing fiction for children. Seeing a gap in the market, she set up her own publishing company (Dernier Publishing) to produce Christian fiction for children and young adults. Dernier is now an award-winning company with a growing number of authors and successful titles. Janet married again in 2011 but keeps her previous name (J. M. Evans) for her novels. In response to requests for help from new authors, Janet also runs write-for-a-reason.com, to equip and encourage writers of fiction for the younger generation.

When Janet is not publishing, writing, speaking, teaching, or dreaming up new plots for stories, she can be found walking in the countryside, spending time with family and friends, and helping at the local Community Fridge.

She lives with her husband and extended family on the very edge of London, where the urban landscape turns into trees and fields.

4

WHY WRITE FLASH FICTION AND SHORT STORIES?

ALLISON SYMES

Flash fiction is generally accepted to be any story which is up to 1000 words in length. Any story above that word count up to about 20,000 words is a short story. Most of the short stories you see in the women's magazines come in at the 1500 to 2000 words mark. My focus is on flash fiction but I write short stories up to the 2000 word mark as well. I'm published in both forms online and in print. For short stories, I have work published in a number of anthologies.

Separately, I have two flash fiction collections published via Chapeltown Books, an indie press based around Manchester, and I am regularly published in online magazines and print anthologies with my short stories. Yet the flash fiction side, which is what I'm best known for, happened by happy accident. It wasn't something I set out to do but flash fiction writing has become the love of my creative life - and again that was unexpected. I hadn't even heard of the form when I began writing seriously.

I responded to a challenge set by online magazine, CafeLit, for whom I'd written standard length short stories, and discovered a new form of writing I became addicted to - not that I've minded this. Flash fiction writing has led to numerous opportunities such as contributing this chapter, giving talks on the topic, taking part in an international writing summit, and giving interviews to name a few. All great fun and even more reason to love the form.

Flash fiction is any story up to 1000 words maximum. Short stories are anything above that word count though between a 1500 and 2000 word count is popular for many magazines and anthologies. I adore writing both kinds of story. The challenges are different, as are the markets, but taking part in both of these has stretched and developed my creativity. I love that. There is no chance of becoming bored. There is also the advantage of knowing which form will work best for my characters, given enough time and practice in writing these forms. I can get to bite at one of two different cherries here and I love that. For one thing, I can get my name out there in differing markets and competitions and in turn that will lead to people checking out what else I do.

At face value, it seems as if I'm making my life difficult in writing to a tight word count so why do it?

There are several reasons. Because it's fun; it's challenging; it gives your imaginative 'muscles' a great workout. I can set my characters wherever and whenever I want. And I do. You're reading someone who has written flash tales from the viewpoint of a mother dragon and about the inside of a ping pong ball - guilty as charged there, I think.

The short form fuels creativity. I have learned to think laterally to get a story across that sticks within the rules of word count but still packs a powerful punch, whether it is to make a reader laugh, cry, or scream. I've written stories capable of having widely differing impacts and that is great fun to do.

And some stories simply work better when they're kept short. I've written an interesting character and situation, but the word count isn't long. Fine, it means I have markets for this work in both the flash and short story sector, depending on whether I've written to 1000 words or more.

I have learned so much about editing when it comes to the short forms of fiction and especially for flash where every word does have to justify its place in the story. Learning these skills has paid off for my non-fiction work. These skills are transferable and make me a better writer and will help you too.

I see flash fiction as precision writing. I am always looking for the mot juste as well as thinking about impact on a reader all the time. That's helpful because, firstly, it means any temptation to keep in purple prose is given the boot. Secondly, the limitation on word count encourages precision in choosing words. Thirdly, it means I am far more likely to come up with a story a reader will enjoy reading because I am thinking of their likely reactions from the first draft.

I am fond of twist in the tale stories and humorous tales. These work well in the short forms.

The challenge of flash fiction is to come up with a story with a proper beginning, middle, and end. Flash fiction is not truncated prose. It must follow standard story structure.

I sometimes write character studies such as monologues and again these work best when kept short because I'm looking to trigger an emotional response to my character by my reader. A short story, and flash even more so, is more likely to trigger that response because the reader hasn't got the time to become bored with your character "rabbiting" on about their life. They tell you what matters, nothing more.

I like to think of novel writing as where you are seeing a tapestry on a wall. You are carried away by the sheer scale of it all. You take in as many of the details as you can and there are many interesting threads to follow. For a novella, you're seeing half of that tapestry. You're still seeing plenty of details, just not as many as you would view in a novel. For a standard-length short story, you are seeing a quarter of the tapestry and you are focusing on the world you can see within that quarter.

But for flash you are taking a spotlight and shining it on one corner of that tapestry. You can't see all the details. That's not the point. What you are seeing are those tiny details and following those threads through in a way you could not do with a novel, where there is too much going on. The big tapestry is literally so big you won't see those tiny details. But there are stories to be told following up those tiny threads and I find this fascinating.

With flash, the focus is on the single most important thing in a character's life. Due to that, I have to analyse characters and work out whether they have a story to tell. I am inside my character's head thinking as them - and that is great. Firstly, it means my author voice is not getting in the way. Secondly, my characterisation skills have been sharpened considerably. That in turn has led to my storytelling skills being sharpened up considerably too because I am concentrating on what matters in moving the story along and nothing else.

The fun of flash fiction comes from:

- Seeing if I can write to such a tight word count.
- Discovering I can!
- Then seeing if I can write to a smaller word count etc.

And if you love creating people, this is the form for you. In addition, you are not confined by genre. I've written historical flash fiction, crime flash, humorous fantasy flash, and ghost story flash amongst many others. I find flash and short story writing liberating which sounds odd given the restrictive word counts but this kind of writing stretches you, the writer.

Focusing on the character, their thoughts and actions makes the story more immediate.

Short form writing has taught me to edit effectively because I am thinking about what I must keep in and about what my readers need to know, and I am not going off at interesting but ultimately unhelpful tangents. I have learned to focus.

Flash fiction shows me what my wasted words are, so those are the first I cut on my initial edit. Mine are very, actually, and that. They actually add very little to that story of mine. I've loved what flash has done in encouraging the elimination of repetitions and those words which don't move the story or characters along. Anything not doing this is wasted.

Flash fiction can be a useful warm-up writing exercise. The great thing is, once you have polished those drafts written for an exercise, you've now got markets and competitions to submit those pieces, so dig out your notebooks, see if you can polish these exercises up and submit them. I've had work published doing this.

I've also found flash fiction encourages the development of 'show, don't tell' in my stories. I have to find ways of showing mood, setting, and genre without spelling everything out. For example:

She wore a red coat. What do you get from that? Potentially interesting character and the coat has to be important in some way, otherwise why mention it?

She wore a moth-eaten red coat. That's better. You now know the character is poor and that coat is important, it could be the only thing she has left. It may have special meaning. There will be a reason why she wears a moth-eaten coat.

Flash has taught me to understand what show not tell means and to develop my craft here.

Also, what was your first introduction to reading? I would

suspect it would be short stories, usually the classic fairy-tales. There is something about short stories that just reaches out to us. I used to love reading childhood anthologies of short stories and it is a joy to be writing my own tales.

It is perhaps ironic a restrictive form doesn't stifle creativity. Far from it - the restrictions encourage creativity to flourish as you learn to think of ways to show us your story. No more reams of dialogue - as all that goes into your story is all that makes the story happen. Your pace also increases.

As a reader, I love it when the author leaves things for me to work out. With flash fiction writing, I get to do that all the time.

When you are short on time, you can draft a flash fiction piece quickly. And you will still have written something you can polish later.

They are easy to use as "adverts" on your website, Facebook etc. I often share a flash story as a marketing exercise. I also create story videos using one and two line flash tales and post them on YouTube, which helps with marketing and is entertaining. More reasons to love the short form.

I do write longer stories too but my flash work, used as advertising, can be a way of drawing people into checking me out on Facebook, Amazon etc.

And, of course, flash fiction gave me a route into becoming a published author with book covers with my name on them. That is such a special moment for any author so naturally I am going to sing its praises. Before that, the short stories gave me my way into being in print.

I found that in writing my first love, what I call fairy-tales with bite (humorous fantasy with a twist), I discovered what else I could do with flash fiction. So, I have ended up writing across more genres than I anticipated, and I love this.

When I want more characters or a sub-plot, then I write 1500 word plus short stories and have a great deal of fun but, for me, nothing beats the challenge of writing to 1000 words or under.

Also, you can experiment with form in flash fiction writing, which is tremendous fun. A recent development of mine, which I hope will make it into a future collection, is to use the same character in linked flash stories. That has been interesting, and I hope to do more of it. I'm always interested in people, so this is a good way to take a character I like and do more with them than just let them star in one tale; yet each flash story stands alone. And I have written flash tales in the form of acrostics. For example:

Acrostic

Allison stumbled across the body on her way home from Slimming World.

Cantankerous as ever, she thought, recognizing the chap she'd walked into.

Really had no consideration for anyone else, even in death, typical of him to still be in the way.

Oh my... I guess I'd better call the cops.

Should've gone home the other way tonight.

Trouble falls into my lap at times, she thought.

Instinct made her look around to see a ghoulish figure behind her.

Crammed her fist into the figure's stomach and bashed it over the head with her bag, nothing but nothing was getting in the way of Allison and her dinner!

Ends
Allison Symes

Not based on real life that one, honest.

I believe flash fiction has taken off in recent years thanks to technology. More of us are reading on screens these days, at least some of the time, and bite-size stories are ideal for this. It is my hope that flash might be a good way into enticing reluctant readers to start off with something "manageable" and then discover they're hooked on reading and go on to read longer works. I read flash and short story collections in between reading novels. They make good appetisers - go on, give them a try. I'll read a novel on my Kindle or paperback, love it, find I'm not sure what to read next so I delve into a collection. By the time I've finished a collection, I know what mood of novel I want to read next. So, I see collections as "refreshments" between novels.

I also think as flash doesn't take long to read, it can and does appeal to those who feel they don't have much time for reading. Flash doesn't commit you to too much in one go. And Radio 2 has had a 500 words short story competition for schools - that is slap bang in the middle of flash fiction territory. So, word is spreading about it as a form. Yet the funny thing is the form is not new, far from it. Think of Aesop's Fables or Jesus's parables in the Bible - the majority come in under the maximum word count limit. Flash has been known as micro fiction, sudden fiction and, my personal favourite, postcard fiction. That makes sense to me because you can picture what you might get on to the back of a postcard and it sums up the format well.

And writers have been playing with the form for longer than you might think. The most famous example is Ernest Hemingway's six-word story: For Sale. Baby Shoes. Never Worn. There is a whole world of story, and sadness, implied by those six words. I understand Hemingway did this for a bet. I hope those who bet against him paid up.

Is it easier to write a novel than the shorter forms? I wouldn't like to judge. All forms of writing take time, need crafting, and editing; but the short forms, and building up publication credits in them, will show others you are serious about your writing and others judge you worthy of being published. Who knows where that could take you? If you can manage a competition win or shortlisting from a reputable outlet, publishers and agents will take you more seriously.

Less is more is the flash fiction writer's motto, but it can apply to the standard-length short story as well. Another huge advantage in writing to these forms is they take less time to complete. Note I don't say they're easier to write. You still need to edit and craft but short stories are bound to take less time to write than a novel. There are magazines who still take fiction, including the online ones; and being published here will help build up your online presence, and assist with establishing credibility.

As a reader, I like being moved in some way by what I have read. Short stories and flash tales mean I can be moved like that more often and they are also a great way to test out an author new to you. If you like their short work, you are likely to love their longer works. And the short form of storytelling is worth celebrating in its own right in any case. I am thrilled at what short form storytelling has done for me.

Author Bio

Allison Symes, who loves quirky fiction, is published by Chapeltown Books, CafeLit, and Bridge House Publishing. Her flash fiction collections, *From Light to Dark and Back Again* and

Tripping The Flash Fantastic, are available in Kindle and paper-back. She also writes for Chandler's Ford Today, Mom's Favorite Reads, and blogs for Authors Electric and More than Writers, the Association of Christian Writers' blog spot.

Website: https://allisonsymescollectedworks.com/

5

WHY WRITE DRAMA?

FAY ROWLAND

That's a great question. Here's another.

How are you going to tell your story, get your message across, share your vision with the world? The usual answer is to write a novel, an informative journal article, or an inspiring poem. But have you ever considered using drama?

Not really. I'm no Shakespeare. Why would I want to write drama?

I'm so glad you asked. We need to get engaged.

What? But we've only just met ... oh, not that sort of engaged.

You want people to read what you've written. And you want them to keep reading. Pretty much the most damning review a book can get is 'Didn't finish'. Ouch! You need to be engaging or your words are wasted.

Sure, sure. I want to write an interesting story, but how does drama help me?

Think about TV adverts. They're the ultimate attention-catching challenge. Imagine you have thirty seconds to make me buy car insurance when I want to go to the loo or make a cup of tea instead. How do you do that? With drama.

Who can forget the tear-jerking Sainsbury's Christmas ad

showing World War I soldiers playing football between their trenches? Or the girl catching a submarine on her fishing line ("I bet she's had her Weetabix") and the 1970s robotic aliens laughing at humans for making mashed potatoes. ("They peel them with their metal knives!") Engaging? Oh, this is the stuff that memories are made of.

Hmmn. Tell me more.

Drama involves us. We humans thrive on human interactions, and drama focusses tightly in on them. There is no room in a script for pages of detailed description so beloved of Charles Dickens. (Don't get me wrong, the boy done good, but when I'm three pages into a novel and we're still on the description of the wart on the end of Mrs Snodberry's nose, I start reaching for the DVD.)

Drama gets a move on. It brooks no delay while the narrator tells you what style of shoe the mysterious stranger is wearing, or how the breeze dances with the dappled sunlight on the heroine's gauzy blonde skirt (poetic though, ain't it?). Your reader moves through time at the same rate as your characters, part of the scene. Drama is an immediate, dynamic form and grabs your reader's attention like Eric Morcambe grabbing André Preview's (sic) lapels and saying, "I'm playing all the right notes, but not necessarily in the right order."

Oh yeah. That was funny. But ... it's kinda gimmicky, isn't it? I want to write something with a bit of weight, a bit of substance, something, y'know ...

... dramatic? Fear not, my fulsome friend. Drama has weighty enough credentials.

Grab 'em by the credentials!

How long do you think novels have been around?

Ooh, ummmn, errr. Not sure really. We've had books for a few hundred years. About that?

Yes, that's not a bad guess. The first proper novel in English was *Robinson Crusoe* by Daniel Defoe, published in 1719.

Really, was that the first? Surely there were stories before that.

Stories, yes, but they weren't novels. They were legends, fables, short stories, or histories. A novel has to be something new (that's what the word means), of a decent length and with a unified story. Robinson Crusoe was the first of its kind.

Of course, that was only the first one in English. The earliest novel anywhere was written 700 years earlier, around 1010, by a Japanese noblewoman. It's called *The Tale of Genji*, and tells of the lives and loves, the intrigues and outfits of Japanese courtiers.

Ah! So, it's like Keeping up with the Kardashians?

Ummn, sort of. Moving on.

The earliest novel is a thousand years old, but we need to wind back another three millennia to reach the first dramas.

Wait a minute. Three millennia? You mean we're going BC?

Yup.

Like The Flintstones?

Not that far. The first recorded dramas date from around 2000BC, to the ancient Egyptians. They performed annual plays about their gods, complete with costumes, characters, and scripts. Unfortunately for some of those early Egyptian actors, directors went for hyper-realism and the special effects departments were somewhat under-developed. One type of play, in which Osiris and his followers are slain by his brother Seth, often resulted in many actors actually dying!

Ooh-err!

Ooh-err, indeed. Other than the gratuitous killing, Egyptian theatre showed many similarities to medieval Europe's passion plays and to modern Japanese anime.

So there really is nothing new under Ra, eh?

Under what? Oh, under the sun. Yes, very clever.

Thank you.

I didn't mean it. I do the funnies round here.

Oh. Sorry.

The Greeks have a word for it

Fast-forward 1500 years and we see the hugely influential Greek theatre emerging like Aphrodite from the waves (but with more clothes on). Think Sophocles, Euripides, Aristophanes, and lots of other people with similar names. European theatre is based on Greek, even to our buildings, with wings, proscenium arch, scenery and an orchestra pit.

Greeks, they're guys who had the masks with the sad and happy faces, right?

That's right, tragedy and comedy, plus a third type that, frankly, I'd rather forget.

You intrigue me. Do continue.

The ancient Greeks used their plays to explore the world they lived in and what it meant to be human. (On a slightly less exalted note, theatre was also the best/only form of entertainment around other than events like the Olympic games. And, let's be honest, there's only so long you can spend watching naked blokes wrestling.)

Ummn, well ...

We use theatre for those same reasons today and we still have the two main forms. Tragedies would take your heart and put it through the wringer. You hadn't really been to a Greek tragedy unless you had got through at least three boxes of tissues and your mascara was dripping off your chin. They called this *catharsis*, cleaning out and releasing your pent-up emotions by having a good old cry.

Shakespeare's *Romeo and Juliet* is a classic tragedy (actually, as is any of Shakespeare's plays where the stage ends up littered with corpses). For modern tragedies, try Steinbeck's *Of Mice and Men*, Russell Crowe in *Gladiator,* or most episodes of *Eastenders.*

Greek comedies were satirical, poking fun at those in power and lampooning the famous, like *Spitting Image* or the US's mock-news *The Daily Show*. Later, the focus of comedies morphed into laughing at ourselves and the absurdities of ordinary life, similar to contemporary sit-coms and *The Simpsons*.

The third type of Greek theatre was the satyr play, which often came at the end of a tragedy triple-bill. These plays featured a chorus of half-goats (satyrs) and were short, sharp, and bawdy. There were boob jokes and bum jokes and farts in abundance, and the actors pranced around wearing large comedy willies – the kind of 'alternative' show that you'd not take your gran to see.

Really? And I though the Greeks were so cultured.

Indeed. You live and learn, eh? Tragedy and comedy have stayed the course, but satyr plays are, thankfully, less popular these days, the shortage of half-goat actors doubtless speeding their demise. And all this is 2000 years before Robinson Crusoe landed on the bookshelves of English readers.

With this lustrous heritage, drama is no poor relation to the novel. It has its own Pulitzer prize-winners and is studied in literature classes alongside poetry and prose. I remember reading Shaw's *Major Barbara* at school, while today's children study *An Inspector Calls* or *Blood Brothers*. Even J. K. Rowling's expansive Potterverse has the script-novel *Harry Potter and the Cursed Child* alongside her novel-format stories.

OK. You've convinced me. Drama is classy (except for the half-goats with the big ...

Yes, yes. I don't need reminding.

Help or hindrance?

Soooo [strokes beard thoughtfully], I guess it's a lot easier to write a drama than a prose story, because I only have to do the speech, right?

Easier? Ummn, yes-ish. But then, no-ish too.

That's not very helpful.

I know. Sorry.

Writing drama is *easier* than writing prose because you don't have the description and movement to worry about.

But writing drama is *harder* than writing prose because you don't have the description and movement to help.

I'm still not following you.

What I mean is this: in drama you are only writing the speech. Other than perhaps a sentence or two at the start of a scene you are not describing your character, how she walks, the nervous twitch of his eyebrow, the smell of cigar smoke as she rounds the turn of the stairs, the familiar tingle as he waits for the door to open – will she be there this time?

Writing drama is easier in one sense because you do not write all of this background stuff, just the speech and stage directions (like the famous 'exit, pursued by a bear' from *The Winter's Tale*). But it's harder in another sense because you still have to paint the pictures in the minds of your readers.

Hmmn, yes, I see what you mean. So how do I do cope with not having descriptions to flesh out my characters?

Fortunately, it's not all down to you. You have help.

That's great!

And possibly hindrance.

Oh.

When you write a novel, the people in it are your babies. Many of us spend hours over character sheets, dreaming up a back story to explain why Nev hates chicken nuggets so much, or fussing over our villain's hair colour. (Go with red, it explains so much.)

In drama, you still need well-rounded characters, with flaws and weaknesses as well as strengths and triumphs, but the final result is only partly your invention. Because dramas contain minimal personal description, the character that emerges is the lovechild of what was in your head when you wrote the script, and how the reader interprets that.

And that brings us to the actors.

It can be fascinating to see how others interpret your work, but also risky. Will the actor 'get' the character? Their idea of your heroine might be very different from how you imagined them, and there's nothing you can do about it if your rugged-jawed, 6'6", leather-clad villain is played by a skinny youth with acne and a Brummie accent who couldn't handle three-day stubble if it were stencilled on.

Taking a positive view of this melding of ideas, it is an utter delight to see the fresh approaches that people bring to your words. In 2020, I wrote a Covid-safe nativity play which was hugely popular, and lots of people sent me videos of their performances. What a joy! A particular highlight was a septuagenarian arriving on a motorbike as the angel Gabriel, with full bike leathers and feathery wings. Fabulous!

The final product of a drama is a mixture of what we, the writers, bring in the form of a script, and what they, the actors, bring in their interpretation. Of course, the 'actors' may be imaginary ones in the heads of your readers as well as real ones on a stage, but the result is the same because, as we know, the pictures are better on the radio.

Painting pictures

Eh? "The pictures are better on the radio"? What's that supposed to mean?

It's a quote. Alistair Cooke, broadcasting legend of the BBC, said, "I prefer radio to TV because the pictures are better".

Ummmn ...

He meant that when we watch things on the TV or in the cinema, the pictures are made for us. They are there, front and centre, in such a way that, after the film, everyone imagines the characters that way. Think of Harry Potter, for example. Harry now always looks like Daniel Radcliffe and Ron like Rupert Grint.

Listening to the radio or reading a drama, however, we have to do more work, bringing heroes and villains to life from only their spoken words, creating the scenery in our heads from the barest of descriptions ('in a park, later that afternoon'), filling the world with noise and smell and texture – and the pictures we make are better that way.

The hero that we, as readers, conjure in our minds is more handsome than any author's description in a novel or any casting director's choice. Our imagined monsters are scarier, our clowns funnier, our canyons more perilous, our mountain-tops more lofty and more glorious. Alistair Cooke was right. The pictures are definitely better on the radio. And therein lies both the challenge and the joy of writing drama.

Plots and plans

OK, so drama is engaging, it's classy and it's not easier or harder, just different. But I'm writing a psychological thriller, not an advert for fizzy drinks or a pantomime, and I certainly don't want to write about the half-goats with the big ...

Don't start that again!

Have you noticed that we automatically look at anyone who is speaking? The same applies in drama.

You want a character-driven story? Then let your characters speak. That's how we get to know people in real life, and it works in storytelling too. The more your characters talk, the better your readers will feel they know them. Let your reader sit alongside the condemned prisoner and hear her last confession to the priest or be the taxi driver who listens in as the world sits in the back of his cab.

I checked last week's TV viewing figures, and top of the

pops is a gritty prison drama. Seven of the top ten programs are dramas, and they're full of people with bad teeth and spots, people who do stupid things and people who make us feel we're not the only twits on the planet. Love them or hate them, the enduring popularity of soaps is testament to the strength of character-driven stories and, oh look, they're dramas.

Hmmn, OK. I take your point. Drama is a good way to tell character-driven stories. You're going to tell me that it's good for plot-based too now, aren't you?

Well, since you insist.

You want a plot-based story with the highs, lows, and stifled screams of a 7-year-old's trampoline party? Get in tight with the action. Lean over the table as the gang plot their next heist. Mingle with the scientists as they discover the instability of their latest isotope. Crouch behind the assassin as she mutters to herself, "This is the last one, I promise."

Concentrating on the speech puts you right in the heart of the action. You are not a distant narrator, surveying the scene from afar. You are a ghost moving among the players, hearing words as they are spoken, then spinning around to see who is whispering behind you.

Drama moves at real time. Speech takes as long to say as it takes to read. One second of script is one second of story. The award-winning drama, 24, famously made use of this, covering exactly one hour of real time in each 1-hour episode.

But perhaps your plot is more funny than fast and furious. Drama is the perfect medium for comedy, providing endless scope for word-play and banter. Ronnie Barker was a master of this form, with hundreds of hilarious sketches including his timeless *Four Candles* ('andles for forks).

Although I sometimes write longer reflective monologues for Easter or Remembrance, most of my scripts are short comedies. *Bert is my Shepherd* retells the twenty-third psalm with a decidedly sub-standard farmer, and *Snottis Green* visits some of

England's lesser-known train stations to think about waiting. A favourite gag is from a sketch about Jonah; on a detour from his holiday in Wales, Jonah finally agrees to deliver God's message and stomps offstage in a bit of a huff. God is left to chat with the Narrator:

God:

[to Narr] Honestly, it's like herding cats sometimes. It's just as well I love the little twerp.

Narr:

Tell me about it. For a prophet he's a bit of a loss!

God:

Ah, we're all human.

Present company excepted, of course.

Anyway, I'd better be off. I need to take Michael to the vet.

Narr:

Michael? The archangel?

God:

No, Michael's the whale – got terrible indigestion.

I think he ate someone who disagreed with me!

Ha ha! I like that – "Ate someone who disagreed ..." Ha ha!

Well, I think you've finally convinced me. I might have a stab at this script-writing lark. Just to see how it goes. Thanks for the suggestion.

You're welcome. I ... ooh-err, what's that?

[exit, pursued by a half-goat with a big ...]

Author Bio

Fay Rowland is a mathematician by trade and has published in the diverse fields of mathematical modelling, theology (both academic and popular), and Bible-based drama scripts. She blogs at The Reflectionary and is a regular contributor to various church resources, with her ninth book due out soon. Fay enjoys knitting and designing labyrinths, and lives in a house full of mess and glue sticks which she blames on the children, but really, it's her.

You can find Fay's books by visiting FayRowland.co.uk

6

WHY WRITE HISTORICAL FACT-BASED FICTION?

JOY MARGETTS

So are you considering writing fact-based fiction? When I first stepped into the world of fiction writing, for me it was an obvious, and perhaps natural choice to write historic fact-based fiction. I'd love to explain to you why, so that hopefully you too can get as passionate about the genre as I am.

I love historic fiction. It has always been my go- to genre. From the first time I discovered books and the joy of reading, I remember being fascinated by stories from the past. Jean Plaidy's books were my first grown up read, followed swiftly after by Ellis Peter's *Cadfael* murder mysteries, and then the in-depth portraits of historic royals by the inestimable Philippa Gregory. I might have even been lured into reading the odd Georgette Heyer regency romance. Include with that the books written by authors who lived in the past: Jane Austen, the Brontës, George Elliot, Charles Dickens and Thomas Hardy. My choice of reading materials was varied, but almost always set in the past. I cannot remember a time when I didn't naturally veer toward the historic fiction shelves in either bookshop or library. And I know why I love historic fiction, and that is because I love history - people,

places, facts and figures, things of the past – they just fasci-
nate me.

Authenticity

What each of my favourite authors did so well was to fill
their writing with well researched facts, that provided great
historical authenticity to their tales. It meant that as a reader I
was transported into the world they had created. I could
imagine myself there, in whatever period of history they set
their stories. It became a form of escapism for me, living with
their characters, in a time far removed from the present. And I
loved it. Of course, all fiction can allow for escapism – sci-fi and
fantasy for example – but there was something vaguely
comforting for me about the world created by historic fiction
authors – it was more real, because it was based on fact. I knew
people actually did live in the way they described, or very close
to it; people just like me. I often longed to be there with them,
especially in the times when the present was not so good a
place to be.

As I matured and my own historic knowledge grew, I appre-
ciated those well researched facts even more. I looked out for
the mention of real persons, places, buildings, and events. They
tweaked my interest and I would want to go away and read into
them further, feeding my own hunger for historic research. I
was so in awe of writers who could successfully write
compelling fictional stories based around real people and
events. I never contemplated, in all those years of loving
historic fiction, that I would one day write fact-based fiction
myself.

The Healing is my debut novel. It is historic fiction, but also
contains a good smattering of historic fact. For example, the
inspiration for the story came when I was visiting the ruins of a
Cistercian Abbey close to my home in Wales. It was a place I

loved and knew fairly well. So, I had my first fact - my story would be set in a real place, not an imagined one. Abbey Cymer is a real place with real history. I could visit the site and see the remains of the church, cloister and other buildings. I could walk around and picture what living there might be like, take note of the situation in which it was built, and the surrounding landscapes. I could research further how the Abbey came to be, what it was known for, how many monks lived there, who the Abbots were, and what royal or noble patronage it enjoyed. I could describe it realistically, using my imagination of course, but based on a good deal of fact.

Within the next hour they had descended a steep hill which levelled out alongside a wide, shallow, slow- moving river. Steep wooded hillsides surrounded them, and just ahead, through some trees, Philip caught his first glimpse of Cymer. He saw the church first, a simply built stone rectangle but rising to double storey height above the other buildings that made up the Abbey. To the southern side of the church was what Philip presumed to be the cloister, with its small gatehouse positioned centrally along the western wall.

It was lovely. Not imposing like Tintern, or surrounded by swathes of verdant green like Cwmhir, but striking enough in its own right. The trees and hills and river seemed to enclose the Abbey like an embrace, shielding it on all sides: like it was a hidden treasure just waiting to be discovered.

The Healing p143

My book actually came from my own experience, and the story it tells is one of healing and redemption. But I did not want to write an autobiography - who would want to read that? Instead, I chose to set my story in another time and place, with created characters and situations different to the ones I had experienced, but close enough that I could use what I had learned to inform their thoughts, feelings and words. This meant that it also had to stand up to scrutiny as historic fiction. I did not want any of my readers to read it and not feel that they were living there, with my characters, in that time and that place, as I had so many times with the books I had read over the years. They had to see, hear, imagine and even smell the atmosphere I was creating. I wanted my readers to literally walk the path with my characters, engaging not just with their thoughts and feelings, but also with the physical things they experienced.

Ready Inspiration

Because of my love of history, my favourite places are ancient sites, whether ruin or abandoned building. I love wandering around and picturing how people lived and worked in those spaces, which I suppose is a form of story creation in itself. So, imagining life in a secluded Cistercian abbey, the sort of people who went to those places for refuge perhaps, was the way my mind naturally went. And suddenly there was a story forming - of a world wearied, wounded medieval knight, finding himself in the care of a Cistercian monk and finding healing, mind, body and soul, within the community of the abbey. My inspiration came from a real place and from a real monastic way of life.

Writing fact-based fiction means that you look to real places, real people, real events for your inspiration. All writers do it to some extent. Even when the genre is fantasy or sci-fi, there are elements of true, factual things that work their way into the stories. A modern crime thriller, for example, based in a specific city, must refer to buildings and places recognisable as that city. That is fact merging with fiction. Perhaps you can think back to your schooldays as I can and remember those far off days of sitting at a desk and being presented with an old photograph and being told to write a story inspired by it. That was fact-based fiction. I have to admit that whilst many of my peers seated around me groaned audibly, I actually relished those kinds of assignments. Perhaps you did too. If, when you can see real things around you, whether photos of the past, or newspaper headlines of the present, you start to imagine a story based around them, then you are well on the way to writing fact-based fiction. You are taking ready inspiration from a fact that has presented itself to you.

The Joy of Research

In writing historic fiction one of the greatest joys for me is doing the research. So much so, that it is easy to spend much more time on the research than it is on actually writing anything. It is so tempting to spend hours reading about the things I want to include in my writing, going down rabbit holes and getting wonderfully distracted.

Once I had my abbey setting, I could also go away and find out more facts about the Cistercian order, what Rule they followed for daily life, what they wore, how their day was ordered, why they sited the abbeys where they did, how they worked the land and supported themselves. If I was going to write about Cistercian abbey life, even though it was fiction-alised, it had to be historically authentic. It wasn't possible to find out everything, but enough to build a framework that was believable. For instance, the monks ate a mostly vegetarian diet, but what that food actually looked like when it reached the table had to be imagined.

Philip could time things by the ringing of those bells. He knew after Vespers that one of the monks would be back with some bread and warm ale for his supper, before they returned to the church for

Compline, and then to bed. They retired as soon as the sun went down during these winter months, and the dark hours stretched long for Philip when sleep did not come. Sometimes they would offer him a draft to help him sleep, but he usually refused. Sometimes they would leave him a candle and Hywel had brought him a beautifully illustrated Psalter to look at. He had taken to reading a Psalm some nights by the flickering candlelight. He could equate with some of those Psalms, it seemed the writer wasn't a stranger to grief, pain, betrayal or despair himself. Morning would come with the sun, although the monks would have been called from their beds in the early hours for Vigils. They would call in after Lauds at daybreak, with his breakfast which was always the same: fresh bread, a small piece of cheese and a cup of warmed goat's milk. Later in the morning Clement would appear with his wash water and clean linens, and then before repairing for his own meal, the monk would make sure Philip had his. Every day it was a pottage made with grains, vegetables and herbs; simple food, but warm and filling.

The Healing p30

Then I discovered whilst doing my research, to my delight, that one of my favourite characters from history, Llewellyn the Great, first Prince of all Wales, patronised Cymer Abbey. They actually bred horses for him there. Now I had a real character to weave into my story. More authenticity. But what about my knight? Who was he? I could have made him up completely, but first I thought I'd research some of the noble families of the period. Then I found the perfect man – Philip de Braose, a member of a somewhat notorious, but well-connected family, with links to both Llewellyn the Great, and to Wales. Conveniently for me I found nothing more about Philip except that he existed, and a few obscure facts about his early life, so he was a prime candidate for me to use. I created an adult life for him, a character, and a history. But my research also meant that

I now had a whole host of interesting and relevant facts about Philip's family and background to add even more historic authenticity to my tale. I loved being able to weave those facts into my fiction; his infamous family, their links with the English throne, and very believable reasons why Philip might have run away to escape his association with them.

'You know some of the history of the De Braose family I presume,'
Philip began, and Hywel nodded.

'You may know, then, of my grandfather William and the atrocities attached to his fame? How my grandfather fell out with the late King John and how his wife, Maud, my grandmother, and his eldest son, my own father, William, were imprisoned and left to die in Corfe castle?' Hywel nodded again.

'I was but a young boy, not yet ten years of age, when they died. My grandfather had already fled to France, and my mother abandoned us and died herself not long after. I was left with my brother John in the care of my uncle, Giles, Bishop of Hereford. We lived in various places, but predominantly here in Wales on the Gower, far enough away that hopefully the King would forget about us. I have only vague memories of that time; it never felt safe and we never stayed long in one place.
The Healing pp 172-173

A perfect framework to build on

There is a wealth of inspiration for story writing in historical research. My inspiration came first from a place, and then from a real person or two. In historic fiction inspiration could also come from an event – a battle, a protest, a murder, a witch dunking for instance. Fascination with the history of a profession, the design of a building, the development of a scientific theory, the inscription on a gravestone – inspiration for historic fact-based fiction can come from all over the place. The sky is the limit.

So, you might start with one fact – that name and death date on a gravestone, perhaps, and then you go and do some research, creating a framework to build your story on. You trawl genealogical websites, county archives, parish records. This is especially satisfying if it is someone from your own family. And then suddenly you find yourself with a whole number of fascinating facts: where they lived, what job they had, who they married, how many children they had. You then engage your imagination, tied in with what you can find out about the time they lived in, and the class they were born into, and a story emerges. You have the *fact* that they died, *fiction* allows you to tell the story of how they died and why. You have the *fact* of where they lived, *fiction* allows you to describe their neighbours and how they interacted with them. You have the *fact* of what they did for a profession, *fiction* allows you to tell the story of how successful or skilled they were, and how they fitted into their community. You have the name of a person as a *fact*, but your imagination can give them a character, make them good or bad, wise or foolish, loveable or detestable. That is fact-based fiction.

I write fact-based fiction because it feeds into the things that I love - history, research, escapism – and because it is the kind of fiction I love to read. Good historic fiction, for me, is always fact based and gains authenticity with the more of those facts it actually contains. But other fiction can be fact based too. I can think of many genres where writers utilise real people, places or events to inspire or add authenticity to their stories. The joy of writing historic fiction for me is that it allows me to read and research a subject that fascinates me. Whatever it is that fascinates you, that gets your imagination going, that inspires you – if it is real, if it is a fact – then use it! Read more about it, research it, collect up your facts, build your framework, and then I encourage you to start writing, your very own fact-based fiction.

Author Bio

Joy Margetts has loved writing for as long as she can remember. A retired nurse, mother of two, and a new grandparent, she also has a lifelong interest in history, and loves nothing better than visiting ancient monuments or burying herself in archive material. She was brought up in the South of England but for the last twenty-five years has made her home on the beautiful North Wales coast, and her writing is inspired by the landscapes and spiritual heritage of her adopted homeland.

More information on Joy and her writing, her personal blog, and the link to purchase *The Healing* can be found here www.joymargetts.com

7

WHY WRITE CAT TALES?

KIRSTEN BETT

You may be wondering why on earth you should consider writing about cats; read on and I will hopefully convince you it is worth considering.

I have always been a cat lover. When I was seven, I persuaded my parents to adopt a ginger kitten even though they weren't too keen on the idea. I loved Ginger but a few years later had to leave him behind when we moved to the other side of the world. Some fifty years later, my partner Wim and I have a black and white tom cat called Max. He is more like a dog: he loves jumping in the tub, gobbles up envelopes from the tax department, and guards our house fiercer than a Rottweiler. I blog about him a bit and no doubt he will shine in his own book one day.

But the star in my first book which will be out this year, is our tabby, Wilma. She tells the story of our emigration from the Netherlands to New Zealand, and back again ten years later. Not many cats could tell such a story, which was one reason I chose to write it. I was particularly inspired by Hiro Arikawa's *The Travelling Cat Chronicles*. The star of Arikawa's novel was

Nana and Nana showed me that a cat protagonist can be just as interesting as a human one.

I have read quite a few cat books, varying from the heart-breaking *Jennie* by Paul Gallico to the Dutch Annie M.G. Schmidt's *Minoes*, which was translated into English in 2017 (*The Cat who came in off the Roof*). In *Jennie*, a boy who had an accident becomes a cat. Minoes used to be a cat. They are both engaging books but the cats are really humans even though they have enough cat traits. Nana, on the other hand, was a proper cat, and yet there was nothing one-dimensional or shallow about him.

Over the years in several writing training settings, I was told not to choose cats as the main characters – they always try to sneak in to my writing - because they are one dimensional and boring. In my research for this article I came across more women who had experienced this. One also said she had been warned off publishing her stories about cats under her real name. I bet no-one said that to Stephen King, Edgar Allan Poe or TS Eliot...

How my book came about

I had been toying with the idea of writing a fictionalised book based on our time in New Zealand, and after reading *The Travelling Cat Chronicles*, I realised Wilma would provide the perfect point of view. She was certainly not one-dimensional as she had developed from a shy homeless kitten to a social, sage cat. This is how Wilma came to mind-speak her story to me:

"Even now Willem seems to suit me more, it sounds more adventurous than Wilma. And I am nothing like that cave-woman on TV. I think a lot. I am sitting downstairs on our couch in Leeuwarden, Friesland, the Netherlands. I am mind-telling this story to my human-lady. She only writes sad poems about our other cat Prince who went to the vet a couple of months ago, supposedly for a few pills, but he never came back.

I am still here, alive and kicking. I mind-speak to my crying human: Dude. I am still with you. I make you happy, write about me. I have had many, many adventures like the cat in the book you just read.

See, I just heard my lady-human talking to my man-human about how good this book was. It was about this Japanese cat called Nana because his tail was in the shape of a seven, nana in Japanese. They went on a road trip. A road trip? I have been in the sky. For days and days. So come on my lady-human, tell my story.

I have been around the world, all the way from The Netherlands to New Zealand with my ginger friend Sailor who sadly came back with us in a little pot. The young man Prince did get to travel back with me but now, only a few years later, he is in a little pot too. It really is up to me to tell our story."

Reading cat books

If you want to write fiction about cats, you'll also want to read cat fiction. See how others do it, see what feels like you. Although I have read quite a few cat books, my research for this chapter showed me that I have some catching up to do. For example, Goodreads has a list of 257 best cat books and Book Riot has a list of the best 100 cat books.

Top on my to be read list are:

- *The Guest Cat* by Takashi Hiraide
- *If Cats Disappeared from the World* by Genki Kawamura
- *The Cat who Walked a Thousand Miles* by Kij Johnson
- *Dewey, the Small Brown Library Cat* by Vicki Myron
- *I am a Cat by Natsume Soseki*

It is remarkable that cats play a huge part in Japanese literature. They are seen to have protective powers and to bring good
luck. Well that certainly applied to Wilma. Her name means
resolute protection. Sadly since she started mind-speaking her
book, she has passed away. I miss her calmness every day. She
was still very much alive when I started writing her book.

Why write about cats

If you love cats as much as I do, you should write about them.
And if you have felines walking about or in the afterlife, you
can even ask them for advice on what to write or do. Their
answers will amaze you. As mentioned, we now have the black
and white Max. In June I took a workshop called *Writing With
Your Pet* from Tawnya Renelle. It was packed with great exercises. For the last one, she asked us to actually write nearby our
pets.

Max was chilling on the mat in the bathroom in the room
next to where I was sitting. He had bolted at the first instance. I
took my laptop and pen and paper to his highness, and laid
down on the mat with him. It was all very undignified. Max
tried to take my pen, bit me and walked off after I had finally
managed it. He then sat on the other side of the bathroom,
staring at all the other people and their more docile pets.

Then Max looked at me. He told me he wanted me to learn
Frisian as he had been born in a Frisian household about 10
months earlier and he really missed the language. We live in
Friesland in the Netherlands. Frisian is recognised as an official
language and is widely spoken. If you live in one of the villages,
it will probably be the only language spoken. I would love to
learn the language especially as Leeuwarden the capital of
Friesland is a city of literature and I miss a lot by not speaking
it.

So even though Max is the most evasive cat I have ever had,

he has already brought me a lot. I just needed to learn to listen. Another reason to write about cats is that they are entertaining and smart - qualities humans might lack. You will never have to search for stories, they will give you several leads on a daily basis.

The only thing I hate about cats is that the chances of outliving them are high. Having had cats for nearly five decades now, I can tell you that final hour, those final days, it does not get any easier. On the contrary. It took a lot of overthinking to decide to get another cat after our last two died so close to each other and one so young. But we decided that a life without cats was just not for us.

If you have lost a cat buddy, I certainly recommend writing about them. You can let them have adventures and it helps deal with your loss, that huge void they leave. I hate it when people say – probably with the best of intentions: "Just get a new one." Would you say that to someone who was grieving a human. Writing can help you through though; also if you let other people read it, people who have lost a loved one as well, they get it. The awkwardness to know if you can talk about your deceased pet yet again is out of the way and in return you could provide some comfort to people who have lost a pet as well.

Your pets also represent different phases in your life. That provides an added bonus if you are writing a memoir from a pet's perspective. Remembering through their eyes can bring things back from the big black void called forgotten. I loved talking about our time in New Zealand through Wilma's eyes because through her adventures the town came to life. Wilma loved the outdoors, she loved New Zealand.

I wanted Wilma to have adventures, she might never have had. Then again, she might have had many more I don't know about. I wanted to look at New Zealand and the Netherlands through her eyes. Writing from a cat's point of view also cuts down to the chase. It helps with more showing and less telling.

I loved channelling Wilma, she let me see my town, Featherston, in a completely new light through her adventures, as in this chapter when she goes camping with her pal Good Looking.

A walk with Good Looking

"Bell Street is beautiful, long and wide, more an avenue. Most streets in Featherston are wide but what makes Bell Street special are the many trees lining the pavement and gardens. Birds love Bell Street; their birdsong is almost deafening most days. But that day it was so hot the roads were melting; you could see the air shimmering above the road. The birds had taken to the hills or were sleeping in the shade of the trees. It would have been silent if it weren't for the cicadas. Cicada-scratching was summer to me. I liked the sound but did not eat them as my digestive system was sensitive already. Prince ate them all the time, he would.

I was happy to be walking on grass, though I did have to cross a couple of streets and avoid the melting bits. I also had to cross the railway tracks. In the weekend not many passenger trains came through and I knew exactly which ones did. I had also learnt to look out for the ones that transported dead trees without any branches. These trains were unpredictable but made a lot of noise. We even heard them from our house when the windows were open. Those trains were nearly as long as Hickson Street.

Because of the heat not many people were about. Just how I liked it. Now and then I got a fright because one of the little humans squealed in a garden or splashed water from their pool over the fence.

Good Looking lived on the corner house right at the bottom of the hill. He is ginormous. I could see his black and white self on the fence as I crossed the last street. His humans made him where a cat sun hat, kind of like an Australian sun hat with all the beads on it against the flies...

"Where is your shadow?" he asked. "Want to come for a real walk with me. None of that pussy pussying on the main tracks. I am going to kill a goat up the Tararuas?"

"Sure," I answered having no idea what he was talking about. We walked and walked, up and down the hills that got more like mountains every paw step. Good Looking did not talk much, he was too busy pouncing around, hiding behind bushes so he could pounce on me. I thought he was funny.

But I was getting hungry. I asked Good Looking if he had any Jimbo's. He ran away, lots of screaming and hissing, and came back with a dead, furry thing between his teeth. A possum, he hissed while he spat out the fur that had got stuck between his teeth. It was delicious. Then I suddenly remembered it could be poisoned.

"Nah," Good looking said. Not here, they are not allowed to drop poison here. They could still do it but when a possum is alive as this one was, it was fine. He almost looked admiringly at the stack of bones that remained on our picnic spot. He asked me if we should go and find some water too.

"Yes please", I said.

"Oooh aren't you the dainty lady?" he joked.

We had a drink at this waterhole. The water was clean and fresh and to my surprise Good Looking jumped in and swam. A swimming cat? Prince would love it here, so I was not going to tell him because he'd never get here alive. A couple of goats were drinking on the other side of the watering hole. They looked too big for Good Looking to take on.

"No skin off my nose," he said. "But I never kill anything with a full tummy." Ha. We were happy and sleepy so we curled up together until the sun had gone down.

It became nice and cool at night. The stars were enormous, we heard some possums cry over the one that died but it didn't last long. "Possums die all the time, they should not even be living here, they are not native."

"Neither are we," I thought and fell asleep again, the best sleep of my life.

How's that for an adventure of a cat who thought her name boring. And all the while I never told her, her name originates from resolute protection in old German, Scottish and Swedish.

As you can see, writing cat tales can be the greatest of fun and challenges you in a way no other type of writing does. This is why I feel you should consider writing in this genre. You won't regret it.

Author Bio

Kirsten Bett now lives in the Netherlands, but she has also lived in New Zealand for large parts of her life. Her partner Wim and she have downsized their life, so they have time to do what they love. Kirsten loves writing. She studied creative writing at Whitireia Polytechnic in New Zealand and is publishing her first book in 2021. You can read more about her work on her website: kirstenbettauthor.com

8

WHY WRITE MEMOIR?

JENNIFER NGULUBE

In many parts of Africa after dinner upon the sound of a tantalising drum, villagers used to congregate around a central fire and settle down to hear stories. The story tellers told many interesting and captivating stories. These stories have always had a ritual for the people of Africa in the evening after a hard day's work. This was a tradition in my family too. l recall growing up in a small African village in Zimbabwe, the highlight of my childhood was always made when we all sat around a big log fire roasting corn and listening to either our grandmother or grandfather telling us remarkably interesting African folk tales. These were very cleverly twisted and made to have valuable life lessons. At the time l did not realise just how important my grandparents were to me in my formative years and in my adult life.

Now lam trying to have a recollection of who my grandparents were, as to what their characters were like. Memories piled up year after year like boxes of unsorted photos. Yet, until something significant happened in my life l did not know what to do with all these memories. Memories are shifty and hard to follow. If you know who you are only through your memories your sense of self will be as tangled as an old storage closet. By creating a written narrative, your past takes shape, offering a clearer vision of who you are today. This is when I really wish my grandparents had written and captured their memoirs for the benefit of my generation in the family and the ones yet to follow. As I am curious about my grandparents there is a good chance my grandchildren will be curious about me and by writing a memoir I have left a legacy that will last forever in my family, the larger community, and the world. Having grown up in the pre-internet era, my childhood was spent in in a substantial monoculture. There was a single shared set of values and beliefs that everyone was expected to conform to. As someone who did not fit into that set of shared expectations I only grew further apart from my peers and this created a substantial sense of isolation and oppression. However, with the ability to communicate instantly and in expensively across the planet, this has given me access to like-minded individuals who have eased that sense of isolation. I can imagine how many more people can benefit from sharing their stories with the world if encouraged to put their experiences on paper.

My love for listening to these stories led to a love of reading memoirs. I remember the excitement I felt the day I first laid my hands on Nelson Mandela's *Long Walk to Freedom*. I was so inspired I could not put the book down as one part of his life led to the next. His struggles, his imprisonment in Robben Island and finally his release after twenty-seven years of his adult life being spent in prison. I walked that long walk to freedom with him in my imagination and celebrated with him in my mind as he rejoiced at his release. Mandela's memoir created a hunger in me to read more famous people's memoirs as I realised how powerful a professionally written memoir is to the mind.

Jeannette Wallis was quoted as saying

'One of the lessons 1 have learned from writing my memoir is how much we all have in common. So many of us think that certain things only happened to us and somehow, they make us less of a person."

She goes on to urge people especially older folks to write about their lives, it gives you a new perspective. In writing your memoir you are handing over your life to someone and saying, this is what 1 went through, this is who 1 am, and maybe you can learn something from it. If you can do that effectively, then somebody else gets the wisdom and benefit of your experience without having to live it.

The next memoir 1 read, and it has left indelible impressions in my mind is the life and story of Coco Chanel. Our backgrounds are different as chalk and cheese, but we have one thing in common. Our struggles as immigrants in a foreign country make me feel so connected to her. Her struggle as an immigrant and facing the cold long winters when she was homeless, her perseverance, the way she went from rags to riches. Having read her memoir, I could see parallels in our lives; as an immigrant myself my own life took different twists and turns, and my life completely turned upside down when I left my home country – Zimbabwe – to settle in the UK. I was unprepared for the long, cold, and harsh winters ahead of me. I found myself homeless somewhere along the line trying to settle into my new adopted country. There were many moments of despair, but there were more lows than highs, and something gave me courage to keep going. I know now that reading other people's memoirs was indeed a blessing to my own life. I often might have thought of Nelson Mandela as someone I knew personally, and I had to remind myself there is struggle before joy. I had to remember Coco Chanel sleeping rough on the cold London pavements in the winter months and that had a very calming effect in my own life as my struggles went on.

Through my struggles I found my love for fostering children from abusive backgrounds. In this job I found my true calling and little did I realise where this job would take me. There is one thing when we work or do something from the heart it shows. I cannot express in words the joy when in 2015 I was awarded an MBE for services to children by her majesty the Queen. For the first time in my life I was forced to stop and take stock of my life. As I sat down and reflected on my story, I knew I had a story to tell the world, a story of struggle, courage, and triumph. At that point I knew it was necessary to start writing my own memoir *Sailing Through the Storms of Life*. This was a memoir of my own life challenges from my humble beginning to the most magical moment of meeting Prince Charles in Buckingham Palace.

Writing a memoir can lead to self-discovery because it gives you a chance to look over life with a more mature perspective. Memoirs can connect with people who have gone through similar experiences or people who can empathise with your story. I have found that reading memoirs has had a long-lasting impact on my life. Whether you curl up with memoirs on a regular basis or pick one up every now and then, you know how powerful their capacity to take you, the reader, for an exhilarating ride. The popularity of women's memoirs is booming. Women from all walks of life are finding their memoirs are a way of communicating and shedding light on experiences that would go unnoticed, hidden in a world dominated by men. More reasons I believe writing memoirs is great.

Orange is the New Black, a memoir by Piper Kerman who wrote about her year spent in a women's prison is not only a best-selling book but also one of the biggest television shows. Another great example of the powers of memoirs *is Call the Midwife* by Jennifer Worth whose story as a young midwife in post war London is extremely popular on television. As much as we sadly lost Maya Angelou, it is heart-warming to see her memoir *I know Why the Caged Bird Sings* which talks about overcoming childhood abuse and trauma, still making it to the bestseller lists long after she left this world. This book has recently hit the best seller list yet again. Such is the power behind memoirs they can keep our stories alive long after we leave the world.

Like all memoirs, my story focuses on unusual experiences as the chapters of the story of my life have the combination of thrills, sadness, survival, and triumph. But more than that, memoirs resonate because of the shared emotive experiences. So, though my story may be unusual or unique, readers can relate to the common things for everyone. These are things such as finding a way to live instead of just existing. Writing your memoir helps you to identify the threads and things in your life and make sense of what you have lived. Writing about your life is a healing and transformative journey.

In her recent memoir, *Becoming,* a work of deep reflection and mesmerising story telling, Michelle Obama invites the readers into her world. She writes about the experiences that shaped her childhood to the years she spent in the White House balancing the demands of motherhood, work, and living in one of the world's most famous addresses. She gives inspiration on different levels as her story can be used to connect with both young women and the older generation of women. Such is the power of a professionally written memoir as it gives the reader an insight into the life of the writer.

Amongst my already mentioned reasons for writing my

memoir I think by writing about your life you connect with those who read your words. Whether they are relatives, friends or even strangers, by connecting with them you reduce isolation and increase the size and intimacy of your network. Writing about your life lets you share ideas and lessons; your wisdom can help others grow and learn with you. I feel by writing my memoir I have contributed to my extended family and the entire culture. All culture accumulates from the creative act of individuals sharing their unique perspective. I found that as 1 wrote my own memoir, I had gone through some experiences that had piled on in my mind and made a hazy and difficult web to detangle. Writing my memoir helped me psychologically as it helped dissolve the hard knotted experiences of loss, betrayal, and regret that had kept me in the dark in the past despite my efforts to forget.

Writing is a challenging mental activity and research shows that mentally challenging yourself helps improve your mental agility and stamina. It is also said that writing helps brain cells to develop. Sometimes we attempt to look at ourselves as one in the crowd and so it might naturally come to you to ask yourself why you should bother writing your story and even wonder if anyone would take time to read your story. That is one of the reasons you should go and tease out the details of your actual path and look for what makes your journey worth reading you will incidentally also reveal what makes it worth living.

For me what inspired me to write my memoir was to preserve my life's special memories - being awarded an MBE and being invited to Buckingham Palace for someone of my background is not something that happens often. This has no doubt created extraordinary memories my loved ones would like to keep. Writing my memoir allowed me to preserve the special memories of events, people and places that have been important in my life so far. Your personal battles are worth telling and learning from. Your stories can be a great source of wisdom and comfort to people who are fighting a similar battle now in time. Writing your memoir and how you overcame challenges can serve as an important inspiration for others. Like it or not our day to day lives and the world are fast paced. Most of us do not stop and reflect on who we are and what has happened in our lives. As a result, we become more disconnected over time with ourselves and the life we have led. Stories are meant to be treasured and shared and Iam encouraging everyone to consider writing their own memoir whether you choose to publish it or keep it within the family the story of your life will always be within reach for your loved ones. Whatever you have done in your life you have undoubtedly done great things and made extraordinary memories that you , and your loved ones will want to keep forever.

Extract from My Memoir

I can understand how likely it is to fall prey to life's difficulties and succumb to its challenges and end up in a phrase of depression and self-pity. Also, l know how much courage and strength one needs to have to emerge out of all problems as a better and stronger person. But what one needs during the most difficult of times is the realisation that change is needed and the ability to change with circumstances. Flexibility and an ability to change are some of those qualities that God has ingrained in the human spirit. In addition to resilience God has also ingrained hope in the human spirit. It is this very hope of finding happiness and a better life in the future that gives humans the vigour to keep going. However, not losing your moral values and ethics in the process of change is equally important. A lot of people do change but lose their morality and ethical values in the process. As a result, they end up becoming soulless monsters.

. . .

As you can see I love writing memoir and I hope I have instilled that passion in you as well. Having read this, is it time to write your story?

Author Bio

Jennifer Lizzie Ngulube MBE is an appointed Member of the British Empire whose story began from humble beginnings in a small African village in Zimbabwe. Jennifer is a published author with an Amazon international bestselling book, a global speaker, and child protective specialist.

You can find out more and buy the book at any online store.

9

WHY WRITE CRIME OR MYSTERY?

WENDY H. JONES

When considering why we are, or should be, writing crime it would be impossible to dismiss the history of the genre. I am going to be bold here and say perhaps the first crime story ever written was when Cain killed Abel in the book of Genesis in the Bible. I give this as an example that humans have been fascinated with crime and its effects since the beginning of time. Edgar Allan Poe is attributed with actually writing the first crime story, *The Murders in the Rue Morgue*, published in 1841 in *Graham's Lady's and Gentleman's Magazine*. Thus started the world's love affair with the crime story. Writers such as Wilkie Collins, Sir Arthur Conan Doyle, Agatha Christie, were quick to follow in Poe's footsteps in what is known as the Golden Age of detective stories. Noir, or dark, crime fiction followed with its popularity continuing to this day.

It was authors such as these who shaped my reading throughout my life and helped me develop my passion for all things crime and mystery. I am not alone in this as the crime genre vies with romance to be the most popular genre for readers in any given year. To give you some insight into just how popular crime books are, they are Scotland's second biggest export after food and drink. *The Guardian* reported in June 2020 that in just one week readers bought 3.8 million print books with crime books topping the chart and I've read another statistic that says one in three of all books read in the United Kingdom is in the crime genre. It is obvious that crime books are extremely popular and one of the industry's largest money makers. What makes these figures so extraordinary is the fact they relate to a period where stores had only just reopened following lockdown. So, I would say this is one of the top reasons why you should consider writing crime – you will have no shortage of readers and the genre will remain popular for many years to come.

Why is crime fiction so popular? Why do readers come back to them time and time again? Why does it continue to dominate the charts? I believe it is because readers can flirt on the edge of danger without being in danger themselves. It helps them to process the grittier side of life and deal with the danger that may, and I stress may here, lie around every corner. While evil things happen in the pages of a crime novel, justice is always served with the perpetrator being caught. This brings a satisfying natural order to the story and thus, by default, to life.

It may also be that the reader sees themselves in the main character or protagonist. They may not be perfect, but they are doing their best; they may often just seem to be bumbling along but somehow, they still manage to save the day. Then, at the end, the reader realises they were not bumbling along at all but actually knew what they were doing. The reader is challenged to follow the clues, follow the red herrings, and solve the mystery for themselves.

What does this mean for the crime writer? What is it about that genre that makes it one many writers turn to time and again? Indeed, why should you consider writing in this genre? A good starting point is that you like reading in the genre. Whilst it is possible to learn to write in any genre without reading it, having a passion for the genre is always a good way of getting off the starting block. It allows the writer to explore the tropes of that genre, to avoid cliches, and avoid breaking the conventions expected of the genre. You may be thinking you have no passion for the genre, but many books hailed as literary fiction have mystery at the core and the same can be said for most other genres. Learning to write crime can help to improve your writing in all genres and give your storylines greater depth and complexity.

Writing crime is also a challenge, that challenge being to ensure that the plot is complex enough to fool the reader yet make it simple enough that by the final denouement the reader is saying, why didn't I see that? On top of this the would-be crime writer may assume that crime fiction is plot driven. This may be true in some crime fiction, but the characters also need to earn their place in the story. They must be well rounded, have some sort of inciting incident, and have obstacles thrown in their way. They must also develop and grow as the story progresses and find out something about themselves in the process. This complexity allows the crime writer to mine the depths of human emotions, not only in the protagonist but in the antagonist and any supporting characters. Death and murder bring out the worst in people and it is this that crime writers can draw on to develop well rounded characters. In my *Detective Inspector Shona McKenzie Mysteries*, I give the killer's story as well as the police story, so the character of the killer is an important part of the book.

The writer can also explore different facets of humanity and the ways in which their characters react given different circumstances.

In which other genre can the writer examine their own character and dance on the edge of criminality without being a criminal? Both readers and writers can flirt with danger from the safety of a notebook, computer, or book. I often say I do the only job which allows me to kill people legally. On numerous occasions I have been asked if any of the people I kill in my books are real? Whilst it would be tempting to kill off people who annoy me, the answer to this question is no. However, some aspects of their character may shape the worst character traits of my antagonist. Revenge is a dish best served in the pages of a book. I am sure many crime writers work in a similar manner.

Often when considering writing crime fiction police procedurals spring to mind. This is understandable, given the plethora of television programmes which litter every channel and the number of police procedurals available on the shelves of any bookshop or library. The sub-genre is endearingly popular. Which leads me to my next point in favour of writing crime fiction. There are numerous, and I mean numerous, sub-genres to be found on the shelves. Here is a list of just some of these:

- Police procedural
- Thriller
- Historical
- Cozy
- Animal
- Cooking
- Knitting
- Gardening
- Libraries
- Bookshops
- Christian
- Supernatural
- War

- Non-fiction
- Classic detective
- Hard boiled
- Noir
- Private Detective

I am sure by this point you get the message. Go to one of the online bookshops or drop into your local bookshop and peruse the shelves. You will be blown away by the sheer variety of what is available. If you want to try your hand at Crime Fiction you do not need to be shackled to the stereotypical story. You can literally start anywhere. This is a genre ripe for exploration and experimentation.

It has been suggested that it is better to stick to the darker types of crime fiction and that cozy mystery no longer sells. Should you follow this advice or not? These are the sort of decisions that you will need to make, so researching is an important aspect of writing in the genre. With regards to dark crime selling better than cozy crime, I have seen little evidence for this recently and I believe that cozy crime may be making a comeback. Having attended numerous conferences over the years the sales of cozies were as brisk as the darker offerings. In fact, cozy crime fiction has its own conference, with *Malice Domestic* which celebrates excellence in the genre becoming more popular every year.

It is apparent that writing crime fiction gives you choice and an opportunity to branch out and experiment with different sub-genres. I have done so, and I have enjoyed every minute of the experience. My *DI Shona McKenzie Mysteries* are gritty police procedurals; my *Cass Claymore Investigates* books are humorous cozy crime and my *Fergus and Flora Mysteries* are Young Adult Mysteries – think *Nancy Drew* and the *Hardy Boys*

meets *Scooby Doo* with its own unique and Scottish flavour of
course. Writing all three of these series has allowed me to
explore different aspects of my creativity and use different parts
of my brain. It started with me seeing if I would be able to write
in the different sub-genres and ended with me enjoying
branching out. Readers love the fact they have different series
to choose from and I pick up new readers who only read in one
of the sub-genres. This also has an impact on profits and thus
the ability to support oneself as an author. Writing within the
crime ecosystem means that I can follow my passion whilst not
becoming bored, thus retaining my creative edge. When
writing about the same characters it is easy to become overfa-
miliar with them which can lead to the stories becoming stale.
Stretching ourselves within a familiar genre can lead to fresh
revelation and storylines for existing series, as well as
producing new and innovative series.

'Great literature is simply language charged with meaning to
the utmost possible degree.'
Ezra Pound

With these words, Pound has zeroed in right to the heart of the
matter. I love this quote and believe it is particularly apposite
for crime fiction. The use of language and the nuances of each
word used can raise or lower the tension or change the way a
character thinks or acts. No work of fiction, or indeed non-
fiction, is as highly charged as the crime genre; it is ripe for the
writer to explore the use of words. That is not to say you should
use over long and unfamiliar words; it means you can play with
the nuances of words to provide shades of light and dark. For
someone who loves words, as I do, this genre provides a play-
park for stretching the imagination.

. . .

Like all types of writing, I believe that crime fiction, or murder mystery, can be a lot of fun. Much of the fun comes from dropping in red herrings and leading the reader down false trails. Many crime writers say that they don't plot out their books in advance because they want to be surprised by what the characters do and the ways in which the story unfolds. For the reader to be surprised, the writer themselves must be surprised. I would agree with this up to a certain point – the writer needs at least some plotting, or the story may not make any sense, or the clues may not lead to the correct killer. Characters can often surprise you and it is worth allowing this to happen. For example, a couple of Russian thugs turned up in *Killer's Craft*, the second book in my *DI Shona McKenzie Mysteries*. They are still there in book seven causing havoc and bucketloads of stress for Shona. In my *Cass Claymore Investigates* series an ex-con dwarf called Cameron McQuilleran, "Quill to my friends," strolled in as bold as brass and informed me he was my new character. He became Cass's sidekick and is extremely popular. These characters bring humour and conflict into the stories which is something all books need, even crime fiction.

It may seem crass to discuss money in a book about creativity, however, it would be remiss of me to ignore it completely. If crime books are one of the most popular genres and consistently top the charts, then it goes without saying that you are more likely to make money by writing in this genre. Now, I cannot say you are going to be rich straight out of the gate, but you do have a better chance of selling enough books to make a living. Whilst one would like to write only for the love of it, we all must eat and pay bills. I love writing crime books, but I am also rather fond of eating, and I am sure the same could be said of you. Having money come into the bank each month spurs many people to keep writing.

In conclusion, I hope this has whet your appetite for all things crime writing. I firmly believe it is one of the most interesting genres and that everyone should try it at some point in their career. There's never been a better time to write crime fiction.

Author Bio

Wendy H. Jones is an award-winning, international best-selling author of fifteen books in five different series, covering readers from childhood to adulthood. These include adult crime, young adult mysteries, children's picture books, and non-fiction for writers. She is currently writing a historical fiction book, the first in a new series. In addition, she is a writing coach, editor, and CEO of *Authorpreneur Accelerator Academy* - a membership supporting authors on their writing and publishing journey - and runs *Scott and Lawson Publishing*. You can find out more at http://www.wendyhjones.com

10

WHY WRITE FAITH BOOKS?

MARESSA MORTIMER

I don't know about you, but I am a fast reader. I'm also a lazy reader, so having to look up a host of references is not something that will happen. I might not even look at the references properly, and instead, skim over sentences that look like this: *Ps 56:3-4, 1Pe 1:7, Mal 3:3.*

I'm also a tired reader (usually), and as such, I struggle with books that require me to think deeply and wonder how this applies to me and my daily life as a woman, wife, mum, home educator, writer, pastor's wife...you name it, the options are endless. The idea of figuring it out through a book, once my children are in bed, makes me feel exhausted already. It also makes me choose to tidy up instead of sitting down with a book.

To me, reading is a soothing, relaxing activity. With not too many free hours on my hands, I do want to choose wisely though, so there are certain things I look for in books. The same goes for writing. I write because I enjoy it. I love to sit down and say to myself, "What If..." then open my laptop and type away.

So why do I write faith books, and more importantly, why

do I think you should do so? There are several parts to this question, and I'm going to look at why it is a helpful thing to do first. I also want to look at why you should write faith stories for others, as well as the reason that I think faith stories are important in general.

Why writing faith stories is helpful for you

Writing is a bit like daydreaming and, like dreams, it's a great way to process our lives. It helps me if I simply plan a character, and maybe a faith question or a Bible verse and I will see where the story leads me. I think about the steps ahead along with the characters, and I have been amazed when they have come to conclusions I wasn't expecting. Often, having a character who is completely unlike me helps. Think about that for a moment. Do you like to read about characters like you or characters who are the opposite?

Whilst writing fiction, it is so much easier to allow presuppositions to come out, maybe through other characters. It helps me, for I don't have to nod and smile and say kind, encouraging things. I can have a character roll their eyes at someone, and say, "How did you not see that coming?" You can make a rude character, or a typical doormat one if you like. In a way, you can allow all your hidden feelings to show through. You can examine them and allow God to work through the characters to change you and shape you. So, I invented Martha, my main character in Sapphire Beach. She is a victim of domestic abuse. She has to come to terms with that, as well as process all that has happened to her over the last few years. How did she not see it for what it was? How could she have let her husband do this to her? Why was she not more courageous? Also, how can she show her trust in God from now on?

I know there are many books written about domestic violence and how to overcome it. Many of those books have been helpful, and they are written by experienced people. As I said before, I prefer to learn through stories. I want to know how things feel and how they should make me react. Having seen the effects of DV in a friend's life, I chose to process my thoughts and feelings in a story. Giving the victim a name, a story and private thoughts helped me. I could picture her; feel her anger at people's clumsy attempts to help her. I could feel her nervousness at loud voices, and rather uncharitably get irritated at her physical reactions to stress. That showed me something in my heart. An impatience, or at least a limit to my patience. A lack of grace towards others who are struggling. If I had read that in a self-help book, I would most likely have dismissed that. Now, writing Martha's next trip to the bathroom in a rush, brought these feelings to my attention.

I felt myself cheering her on as Martha fought her fears and tried to trust God more in everyday life. I also cringed when she misunderstood what it meant to be courageous. It was an encouragement to me as well. I enjoyed exploring what courage looked like for me, and where I should leave matters in other, more capable hands. Writing about Faith helped me to understand what trust looks like on a dark day, and how being courageous doesn't mean throwing out common sense.

Writing faith stories can be such a help for us. When people say, "Imagine what it's like to...", you can be so much more involved if you write their story, rather than a clinical list of characteristics. So here is a little exercise for you. Think of a character trait you are struggling with. Maybe you find it hard to picture 'discerning' in a practical setting. Think about what it means. Next, think of a character. Imagine everything about this person that you can: looks, attitude to life, age and at least one annoying habit. Decide whether the character is going to be discerning, or whether you are going to help this person to become more discerning. Picture the setting. "What happens if or when..."

Why write your story? Have you seen the list of books available? That's not the point. You are unique, your faith is unique because your relationship with God is unique. Therefore, your journey alongside some chosen characters will be personal to you. Think of the kind of books you enjoy. Do you like complex books with many characters doing their own thing? Or soothing books; books about people coming to faith? Then you might want to start with that kind of faith story. Some stories might be too close to home. My children are adopted, and so far, I haven't done any fiction related to this. It's too personal. Others might find this very cleansing, so don't feel pushed into a particular story. It is your exploration of your faith.

Why faith books can help others

When you write stories of faith, it helps readers. You might not like the idea of others reading your stories yet, or you might have been published regularly. Either way, it's great to think about the kind of people who might benefit from your writing. Maybe there is a point you would love to make. Maybe there is a Bible verse you would love to share or an encouragement for others. Writing a fictional novel is a wonderful way to share this with readers. Not only might it reach people who would walk past a self-help book, feeling they don't have the energy for more lectures. It is also a gentle way to share with others who might not understand what we're trying to tell them. After all, it's just a story, just a cosy book to curl up with at the end of a long day.

When people can invest in a character, it is so much easier to understand feelings and see where the character is coming from. A problem is no longer somebody failing at life, it is relatable, and empathy is easier to find. Addiction is no longer a weakness, but something that goes much deeper when we struggle along with a character. Forgiveness is no longer something good people simply do, but we can feel the struggle when a character is hurt. By sharing your message in story form, it can be more relatable and accessible to people. There is a danger that the story gets lost in the message, which people will realise soon enough.

Faith fiction is helpful to people around us as well. There are many misconceptions about faith. To me, writing faith fiction is better than writing a tract that people might not read, as they're convinced, they know what you believe. Non-believing friends and neighbours might struggle to understand parts of our lives, and to see it in a story is helpful. It's not as confronting as you trying to explain 'forgiveness' to friends. It is a great way to open up a conversation. Especially when you have focussed on the storyline itself and brought faith into it in a natural way.

Why I think faith stories are important in general

Different people have different views on faith in fiction. Sometimes it's a minor undercurrent in a book, whereas I enjoy books where faith issues are a major part of the story. When starting a faith story, sit down and think about the role of faith in your story. Is the story more about the message or about the adventure, history or crime? For me, the danger in this lies in making it about the message and neglecting the story. My books do have a message, but only because I think, "I wonder what would happen to a character if..."

I have always loved fiction, even as a very young child. It is my preferred way of learning. I love curling up with a book, my mind drifting off to unknown places and eras, and drinking in the information. As a believer, it is also my preferred way of learning about God. I know, some of you will gasp at that, and maybe even think it proof of a very shallow mind. I didn't say it's my only way of learning, just that I prefer it. I love books with characters who are real. Someone being knocked out, who gets up after ten minutes with life carrying on as normal...wonderful idea, but not very realistic. We adopted our children eight years ago, and many people are surprised to see that some traumas are still firmly in place. It's one of the messages I tried to share in Sapphire Beach, for trauma isn't easily forgotten. You can't simply say a prayer, and your memories are healed. Trusting God is easier said than done.

I feel faith fiction is important in this. Faith is my life, God is my Lifegiver, and other Christian characters should reflect that. Does that mean all your characters are going to be sweet, diligent and ridiculously happy? That's not a reflection of life, sadly. Maybe your character struggles with this? That would be a great story to share. Maybe your character has no desires to become a Christian, as they feel the ones they've met have been irritating. I love reading characters like that. They make me feel accepted. They are people I can identify with. When they slam their door so the windows rattle, I sigh with relief, maybe feeling smug that at least I haven't done that. Not today, anyway.

My children love reading books where the family says grace before the meal. Their delight reminded me how important it is to have books available that we can identify with. We can feel marginalised in certain areas of society, but what if your character felt like that, but instead of accepting this, stepped forward in faith? What would happen? What if...

Of course, there are many types of faith fiction. Many Christian novels are historical fiction, although I wonder if they were written because that time seems more natural for faith to be included? I do enjoy these, as I feel it's a great way of learning about history as well as faith. Then there is Biblical fiction, where the book centres on Bible characters. My favourite is a mix of these two, written by Liz Curtis-Higgs, set in Edinburgh in Bonnie Prince Charlie's time, but depicting the Bible story of

Naomi and Ruth. I found these books so helpful, for the story of Ruth is familiar, so when reading the Bible narrative, it's hard to feel it's relevant. To see it in such a new context was incredible. Even when your readers are familiar with the concept, telling it in a fresh way, with unique characters, can be very helpful.

On the other hand, our lives are now, in this setup. That is why I do love contemporary fiction. It can be set in a different world, but the issues can still be the same. My favourite series is the O'Malley Series by Dee Henderson. The way each character comes to faith is so well written. They all had a solid reason for not being a Christian, and she wonderfully deals with this. There are no glib answers, just a careful unpicking of lives, thoughts, and words. I did a similar thing in *Walled City*, where people aren't thronging to receive the Word, and Gax isn't making converts left, right and centre.

What role does faith play in your life? These are my three main reasons why you should write faith fiction. Allow your heart to be helped by it. Write that story about that little thing that's working at your heart in the background and be blessed. Use it to help others. Encourage other believers, give them a relaxing read that is enjoyable and that they can identify with. Write that faith fiction story because faith is part of life, God is our Life and our Light; shine this light the way it should be wherever your character goes. Even if that character fails at their calling, that's life too.

Author Bio

I grew up in the Netherlands and moved to England soon after finishing my teaching training college. Married to Pastor Richard Mortimer we live in a Cotswold village with our four children. I'm a homeschool mum, enjoying the time spent with the family, travelling, reading, and turning life into stories. I want to use my stories to show practical Christian living in a fallen world. You can find out more at:

https://vicarioushome.com

WHY WRITE IN YOUR THIRD AGE?

NANETTE FAIRLEY

The English historian and founder of the Open University and U3A*, Peter Laslett, split our lives roughly into four parts:

First Age: dependence, socialization, immaturity, and learning
Second Age: independence, maturity, responsibility, and working
Third Age: personal achievement and fulfilment after retirement, and
Fourth Age: final dependence, decrepitude, and death

I don't know about you but I am keen to stay in my Third Age for as long as I can. Think about all the benefits of your Third Age – the wisdom of a longish life, resilience grown from life experience, flexibility, and hopefully health and well-being. But most of all *time*. Time to keep learning, to be curious, to develop deeper relationships, perhaps to travel and... to write.

OK so you've not written more than an email or ten in the recent past. I know when I left full-time employment, I had not written anything more than emails and business reports for the past maybe ten years. I am ashamed to say I hadn't even written a letter to someone. Snappy, catch-up emails with friends, yes. But more creative and 'interesting' writing, definitely not.

I was a nerdy bookworm at school. Often deeply affected by the stories I was reading, transported to another time or place – far from the small mining town in which I grew up. As a young adult I moved into self-help books. Not the spiritual ones, or the ones about making money. But those that promised I could achieve it all if I just focused on my productivity and increasing my skills. And now, with my full-time career in the rear vision mirror, biographies and autobiographies - both books and essays - are often my read of choice. As I started to find some of my new purpose in writing, my self-doubt always hovered around, but that is a whole other chapter.

Let's not focus on the fact you don't *think* you are a writer just now. Let's focus on why you might *want* to write at this time of life. As you can see from this book, there are many different genres of writing, but I want to focus on writing your story, or that of a family member. Whether that be an autobiography or biography of sorts, more of a family history, or a series of essays about specific events or times. Some examples I have read or wished I had read include:

- Recently I read a truly captivating essay written by a woman who found a pile of love letters from the 1960's - eight years' worth in fact - in her ninety-one-year-old fathers' possessions when he passed away. The letters were not from her mother who had died several years earlier. The essay explored what she found out about her father that came as a bit of a shock, enabled her to explore her feelings about the discovery and ask why he had left them for her to read, rather than destroy them. Perhaps for her to know him better?

- Another example is a little closer to home for me. Both of my grandfathers, neither still with us, had interesting lives in very different ways. One transcribed morse code during the war and later was responsible for allocating postcodes for a large chunk of Queensland, Australia. The other worked in the Ambulance service and befriended US and Australian soldiers stationed nearby, many quite homesick, during the war. And don't get me started on the stories my grandmothers might have told – beginning with having six kids each. Unlike the example above, these stories will disappear when those who remember them can no longer recount them.

'If there's a book that you want to read, but it hasn't been written yet, then you must write it.'
Toni Morrison

While you might have the time now to explore writing, it can be a difficult task if your 'why' is not clear. Why might you want to write? Or write more, in your Third Age? Why choose one story to tell over another? What will you get out of it? How will others benefit? If your 'why' is not powerful enough you may stop before you have truly started.

You need to find your own why and here are some that have motivated others to give time, effort, love and persistence to their writing.

- Every family has history worth preserving. This will be particularly poignant if you are into genealogy and have researched much wider than the easier to access stories from immediate family members. Writing down what you have found will preserve your research for future generations.

'Preserve your memories, keep them well, what you forget you can never retell.'
Louisa May Alcott

- The research and writing of family stories, or your own story, will add to others knowledge of your family. While grandchildren may yet to be born, there will be a time in their lives when this knowledge becomes relevant and important.

'Life has to end, but stories live forever.'
unknown

- Writing can bring you meaning and purpose. Sometimes, post retirement when you no longer have a job title, you can lose your identity somewhat. Taking up researching and writing of your own story or that of other family members, can contribute to what's next for you after full-time employment comes to an end.

- Staying curious and getting your brain to work in new ways is good for you physically and mentally

and can improve your neuroplasticity.
'Neuroplasticity' is the brain's ability to restructure or rewire itself when it recognises the need for adaption. In other words, your brain can continue developing and changing throughout life. To stay healthy and happy we need to continue to grow and learn in our Third Age. Writing can make a wonderful contribution.

- Getting your story down can also be healing – like the practice of journalling can be therapeutic, writing your life story, or the difficult and challenging parts of it, may also help.

> 'Tears are words that need to be written.'
> Paulo Coelho

- Writing your story will also help you remember things. We all know our memory is not always as sharp as it once was as we age. Recently, for the first time in more than 15-20 years I reread my travel journal from my gap year overseas when I was nineteen. It was joyful to remember people and places I had not thought of for years. I laughed at my younger self at times – my crushes and things that offended me then. I also got to acknowledge how far I had come in the intervening thirty-five years. It will be interesting to see what I think of my fifty-year-old self in my mid-eighties if I have the privilege of living that long.

> 'We write to taste life twice, in the moment and in retrospect.'
> Anaïs Nin

- Another reason you may want to write your story is to make sure it gets told in your words, and in your way. No one knows you and your experience better than you.

- Your writing can also help your kids and grandkids understand better who you are and what your 'special sauce' is. In our busy lives many of our interactions are superficial and efficient. Writing is a tool that enables a deeper dive into what makes you, or someone you are writing about, tick.

'There is no greater agony than bearing an untold story inside you.'
Maya Angelou

- Your kids and grandkids will understand more about where they have come from, and this can be helpful in supporting them form their own identities or understanding things that may not have been clear in the past.

- Could you use your writing as an opportunity to leave behind personal advice and learning that may benefit others in your family? Your experience, knowledge and wisdom learnt over several decades is valuable, even if you don't yet see that yourself.

- Maybe you want to use your writing as an opportunity to relive your childhood by writing your childhood memories down. It could be a great way to build a stronger bridge with your siblings, getting them involved in the walk down memory lane.

- I was once encouraged to write down my regrets, hardships, disappointments and failures and then throw my written pages into the fire. That was weird but somewhat cathartic. As valid a reason for writing as any other, I think.

- Perhaps you have done a lot of travel in your Third Age and you want to share the wonder and learning from the experience. What you learnt about a new culture and its people and your thoughts on what you found in each new place. Recently, I travelled to Socotra off the Yemeni coast. I met a very interesting woman who spoke no English, but was so very keen to communicate with me. With effort, I understood her very first question to me. Not where are you from? Do you have any kids? Not the kind of question I normally get, but "What contraception do you use?" I reflected on that conversation in a recent blog I wrote and mused on how grateful I was to have always had a choice in this space.

- Writing can also be very private, personal, and just for you. For example, writing down things that you wished you'd told people who have now gone from your life.

- One of my friends, Edwina Brocklesby, founder and CEO of the Silverfit charity in the UK and, at 78 years old, Britain's oldest Ironman competitor, wrote a book about her story. Eddie didn't start running until she was in her fifties and actually had to learn to swim before competing in her first triathlon. Her book, *Irongran*, has inspired many older people to become more active later in life. Could your story be inspirational to others?

- For some, the act of writing a story, is just plain fun. It brings joy, deep satisfaction, and that positive energy that helps us thrive. Our Third Age is definitely about doing more of the things we want to do, right?

- And finally, you might simply want to entertain others.

And if you think you are too old to write anything, then this roll call of older writers who were actually published (and that may not be your goal) may surprise you.

A quick search through Google, tells me that Brit, Bertha Wood had her first book, *Fresh Air and Fun: The Story of a Blackpool Holiday Camp* published on her 100th birthday on 20 June 2005. The book is based on her memoirs, which she began writing at the age of 90. You may not know that:

- James A. Michener wrote forty books after he turned forty
- Bram Stoker wrote his first novel at fifty and published *Dracula* seven years later
- Pulitzer Prize winner Annie Proulx, author of *The Shipping News* and *Brokeback Mountain*, was fifty-seven when she was first published
- Frank McCourt, who also won a Pulitzer Prize for his book, *Angela's Ashes*, was sixty-six when his book came out
- Co-creator of the Mr Magoo animation, Millard Kaufman, wrote his first novel at ninety

- *Robinson Crusoe*, was Daniel Defoe's first novel when he was fifty-nine
- Laura Ingalls Wilder, author of *Little House on the Prairie*, was sixty-five when her first novel was published
- And finally, the author of one of my favourite books from childhood, *Watership Down*, Richard Adams, was fifty-two when his debut novel came out. Twenty-five years later, he wrote the sequel.

So, what's your why for writing in your Third Age? Do you resonate with any of the ideas outlined here? We all have stories to tell, history to record, things to remember. We may want to offer help or inspire others. Perhaps we want to heal ourselves, entertain or just have fun. Once you find your why, welcome to the wonderful world of writing with the experience, wisdom and courage that often comes with one's Third Age.

Author Bio

Since leaving full-time employment in 2019, Nanette founded WhatNextology, a resource for those wanting to make the most of their life after full-time work and family commitments. WhatNextology provides community, support, ideas, and inspiration for those planning their what's next. She can be reached at nanette@whatnextology.com and to find out more visit www.whatnextology.com.

Notes:

*U3A - University of the Third Age

12

WHY WRITE SCIENCE FICTION AND FANTASY?

ANDREW CHAMBERLAIN

How do you react to the idea of reading a science fiction and fantasy story? Does the thought pique your interest and make you curious for new and fantastic worlds? Or does it all sound like childish nonsense, the province of geeks and nerds?

Your reaction to the idea of consuming any kind of content in the fantastic genres – books, films, or TV – will give you some idea of how you might fare if you decide to write something in one of those genres. Putting it bluntly, if the idea of consuming this content doesn't inspire you, then you're never going to have the desire and enthusiasm to push through and write the 80k, 100k or 150k of words required for a fantasy book.

If that hasn't put you off, then please do carry on reading. In this chapter I'm going to explore the allure of the fantastic genres and give you some tips to help you determine whether this really is an area where you could be exercising your writing talents.

We should start with some scope and definitions. In this chapter I refer to the 'fantastic genres'. These encompass science fiction, fantasy, horror, and all of these sub-genres. But more scope for this chapter will be fantasy and science fiction.

Even within these two main branches of the fantastic there is scope for a wide array of sub-genres. Science fiction has spawned first contact, space opera, military Sci-Fi, and cyberpunk, to name but a few. Fantasy is also a broad palette with high fantasy, gothic, weird fiction, Grimdark, and magical realism.

There's plenty of room in the fantastic genres tent, and so there might be room for you as a writer to exercise your talents. But how can you be sure, or at least, how can you be more sure?

Let's start to answer these questions by looking at the possibilities that science fiction can offer a writer.

To boldly go - the enduring appeal of science fiction.

Recently I was asked what someone should do to work out whether they are interested in writing science fiction. My answer more or less was: 'go outside and look up at the sky' by which I meant go out on a clear night look up and then try to discern what you feel about the things you can see.

What can see when you do this exercise is the panorama of the planets, stars and other celestial features that are visible from earth. If you are exceptionally lucky you might even see the trail of dust and stars that forms part of our galaxy. If you happen to have a good pair of binoculars or even a telescope, you might see a whole lot more than this.

Looking at the heavens creates different responses in different people. Some may feel a sense of mild curiosity, others indifference, and still others might be filled with that sense of wonder that drives the spirit of restless adventure in humanity. If you look up into the skies and feel a sense of wonder in the fact that the light you see may have taken countless millennia to reach your eyes, then that's an indication that science fiction might be the way forward for you.

Of course, a sense of wonder is subjective, and there are

people who think that as our scientific knowledge grows, the awe we feel from looking at the stars will diminish, that our knowledge will take the magic and majesty from the heavens.

I don't think this is the case. Rather, I think our growing knowledge might serve to sharpen our curiosity, our amazement at the heavens, and our spirit of adventure. Being aware of the distances to the objects we see doesn't rob them of their mystique. Knowing that the most ancient sources of light humanity can detect in our still expanding universe are nearly fourteen billion years old may add to the sense of wonder that we feel, not detract from it.

Our universe is estimated to be about forty-six billion light years in diameter. If that fact excites you at all, then maybe writing science fiction is for you. If you are also excited by the fact that forty-six billion light years translates into around 28.5 gigaparsecs, then maybe writing science fiction *really* is for you!

It was this sense of awe and wonder that I wanted to capture in the prelude to my first contact novel, *The Centauri Survivors*. The story opens with an astronomer looking out from the summit of a mountain in Chile. The clear air makes this location one of the best places on Earth to observe the stars. The astronomer stands in front of one of the great telescopes at the top of that mountain and looks up at the stars. Here's a short passage from that prelude:

Marcel Dillon stood with his back to the telescope, the dark wings of the dome open wide to expose the illuminated structure beneath. His hands cupped the steel mug of hot coffee and he shivered as the summit wind whipped at his jacket. He glanced across the concourse to the arid slope of Cerro Armazones sweeping away in darkness, and then he leaned back, and looked up through the clear air to the starlit trail of matter that made up the local arm of the Milky Way.

"My God," he whispered into the frosty air; "look at it; we must go there."

Science fiction writers of a certain kind feel that need to

explore the universe. At least in our imaginations we must indeed 'go there'.

This desire to explore runs deep in the genre. We are beguiled by the idea of visiting 'the other': other places, other intelligences, other versions of ourselves. All of these concepts have been explored throughout the history of the genre. We see it in Mary Shelley's *Dr Frankenstein* as her protagonist tries to create a new type of human. We see it in the work of H G Wells as his Martians attack the earth, and we also see it in the prophetic, imaginative works of George Orwell, Ursula K. Le Guin, and Philip K. Dick.

It is this longing, articulated in a million different ways, that inspires science fiction authors to write the stories of exploration and imagination that are the hallmark of the genre. But these great science fiction stories don't just point to something 'out there', they also point to something 'in here', that is, inside us. They point to a truth about what it means to be human, or to be a society.

The best science fiction stories contain within themselves the hallmark of all great stories, and that is two arcs, two journeys. One is external and is manifest in the outward story, the plot. The other story is internal, the arc of the characters, how they develop over time, how they deal with the challenges they face, and how they reflect the nature of humanity.

Within the fantastic genres science fiction provides not only an excellent context for us to express our desire for adventure and exploration, it also gives us the perfect crucible in which to look at ourselves, at the challenges of what it means to be human, to have an identity, and to discover what that identity is.

But we don't have to base our stories in science or even the allusion of science. Just as there are truths to be found in science fiction, so there are also truths to be found in the truly fantastical tales that have been told since the dawn of humanity. Even if science fiction doesn't grab you, it might be that fantasy will.

Parsing reality– the power of fantasy in history and today

Science fiction has a history spanning hundreds of years, but fantasy can claim to have roots in the dawn of storytelling, it is as old as the tradition of humans coming together around the fire and telling tales to each other.

We should not be surprised that the first stories ever told were full of what we would consider to the be tropes of myth and fantasy. These are what helped our ancestors to explain and identify the unknown, to confront the nameless fears, and to start to give meaning to an otherwise chaotic and hostile world.

For thousands of years humanity has wrestled with forces that seem both powerful and inexplicable, and the truth is we still do. We have lived with the constant challenges of the physical world around us; the problems of finding food and shelter, of defending ourselves against predators, of sheltering from the natural forces around us. Since the dawn of humanity people have been terrified and inspired by the great natural canvases that exist in our world: the depth and scale of the great oceans, the wonder and majesty of the constellations in the sky, and the weather in all its unpredictability and power.

Myth, legend, and fantasy have been the tools that we have used to help ourselves parse the world around us, and to deal with the physical and psychological challenges of life. In telling these stories, humanity has made champions out of those who confront and overcome the fierce and fickle world, our adversary in all its forms. We have celebrated the heroes, real and imagined, forming the stories of their lives into what may be the oldest trope in storytelling, the hero's journey.

This is the journey we want to complete for ourselves, or at least see the hero complete on our behalf. We want to see Beowulf defeat the troll-like Grendel, and then take on Grendel's mother, and then finally that arch-trope of enemies: the dragon. We cheer on as the demi-god Hercules slays the many-headed hydra, captures the Cretan Bull, and steals the golden apples of the Hesperides, another feat which involved killing a dragon. We are engrossed as Sinbad sails the oceans, confronting sea monsters, goddesses and all manner of other aquatic adversaries.

These stories span hundreds and even thousands of years and still they have the power to beguile and capture us. For all our knowledge and sophistication, we still we want to see the ascent and triumph of our heroes. Their identities change, as do those of their adversaries and the prizes they fight for, but the fundamental elements of the story remain the same.

You might think that our growing scientific knowledge, and increased understanding and control of the world around us might limit the potential for fantasy to provide inspiration to us all. But like science fiction, this is not the case. We still fight, we still dream, we still recognise the adversary, outside of us, and within ourselves. We still crave stories that put us, or our champion, against these adversaries. All of this may or may not inspire you. But as a writer, how do you know whether a fantasy story is something you should try?

Just as with the science fiction genre, there are indicators that fantasy might be the right place for you to exercise your authorial talents.

If you enjoy the idea of creating magic systems that are grounded in plausibility, then fantasy might be a good choice for you. If you enjoy the idea of creating characters, communities and societies that are founded on principles that are similar to the human experience but also incorporate some fantastical elements; then again, the fantasy genre might be right for you.

If you want to explore the unusual, the bizarre, and the weird, there's a fantasy sub-genre for you as well.

The fact that most of us are not worried about predators, and don't rely on the communal fire for warmth and protection has not dampened our enthusiasm for fantasy, and interest in the hero's quest remains as strong as ever. The Harry Potter series is a version of the hero's quest and is a powerful example of how myth and fantasy still hold a strong appeal for contemporary audiences.

In all their long histories the fantastic genres have never gone out of fashion, and I don't believe that they ever will. The tropes which feature in these stories still appeal to us, the psychological attraction of these tales remains as valid as it ever was. We still want to see our heroes overcome the terrors and challenges that confront humanity, we still want to see the human spirit triumph in adversity, and we still want to assuage our thirst for other worlds, other places, both "out there" in the beyond and also deep within our own identity.

For the aspiring writer, these genres offer a rich vein, *if* they capture your interest. If the fantastic genres grab you, then you're got! But if these stories seem like childish fairy tales or pointless yarns about little green men or women, then steer well clear, it's unlikely that you'll be able to summon the enthusiasm and the discipline to write in these genres.

That said, if you feel that sense of awe, if your heart stirs, if you dream dreams, then give it a go.

Author Bio

Andrew J Chamberlain is an author and writing mentor. He is a hybrid author, publishing books and short stories via the traditional and indie routes and is the host of *The Creative Writer's Toolbelt*, a podcast that gives writers practical advice and encouragement on the craft. In September 2017, he published *The Creative Writer's Toolbelt Handbook* a compilation of the very best advice and insight from dozens of professional writers, artists, and editors, from the podcast. His latest novel, published in July 2019, is *The Centauri Survivors*, a first contact adventure set in the Alpha Centauri system. His Christian supernatural thriller series, *The Masters Series*, comprising two books: *Urban Angel*, and *Cain's Redemption*, was published in 2021.

13

WHY WRITE HUMOUR?

WENDY H. JONES

It is widely accepted that humour is good for both your physical and mental health and it's been said it can also make you more attractive to the opposite sex and more acceptable as a leader. It is true that a well-placed humorous phrase can deflect anger or get a point across more gently. We use humour every day in our interactions with those we meet, and we laugh at the humour we see in or hear from others. Laughter is natural and is so full of healing properties that it is actually prescribed in many hospitals.

This is all very well I hear you say, but what does all of this have to do with writing? I agree, let's get to the point - what does humour have to do with writing? The short answer is, all the above.

Let's start with a little literary humour to get us in the mood.

. . .

A man walks into a bookstore. "Where's the self-help section?"
he asks the clerk. She shrugs and replies, "If I tell you, won't
that defeat the purpose?"
Anonymous

Now this may have you rolling in the aisles, or you may not see
the humour in it at all. Which brings me to my first point when
writing humour – not everyone finds the same things funny.
This brings challenges to the would-be humour writer. Do you
aim for the lowest common denominator hoping everyone will
find something funny in your narrative or do you seek a specific
audience? My advice would be to write the type of humour you
enjoy and write for readers who enjoy similar humour to you.
This will make it easier for you as it will come naturally. Now,
I'm not saying you cannot learn to write humour, because I
firmly believe you can, but if you find what you are writing
funny then you can bet your dear departed granny on the fact
so will others.

Before writing humours books or stories, it is first necessary to
read widely in the genre. I love Janet Evanovich's *Stephanie Plum*
series and they literally have me laughing out loud. Sometimes in
places where the people around you think you should be carted
off to the funny farm for real. I had this experience on a train
where I actually had to stop reading as I was disturbing the other
passengers. Evanovich books, whichever series you read, are a
madcap caper. They are littered with crazy characters who have
absolutely no clue what they are doing and gazillions of exploding
cars. Stephanie, who is the main character, is completely over-
shadowed by Grandma Mazur and Lula, an oversized ex-prosti-
tute. They are so over the top that the caricature is hysterical.

I love these books so much that I thought I might try a Scottish version, without so many exploding cars of course; Dundee, where my books are set is quite a small city and I'd soon run out of cars to use. So, I went back to the drawing board and *Cass Claymore Investigates* was born. Cass is a red headed, motor bike riding, ex-ballerina, who inherits a private detective agency and accidently hires an ex-con dwarf and an octogenarian. She has no clue what the heck she is doing, and the humour arises from this. Quill, her ex-con sidekick, manages to help her with his ever-changing cast of friends, all of whom he met in prison. Plotting this out was so much fun and I was able to be as over the top as I wanted. I basically chucked everything at it in the way of humour that I could think of. Here is the blurb for Antiques and Alibis the first book in the series.

'Cass Claymore, a red headed, motorbike riding, ex-ballerina inherits a Detective Agency, and accidentally employs an ex-con dwarf and an octogenarian. Hired by a client who should know better, Cass has no leads, no clue, and a complete inability to solve a case. Still a girl needs to eat and her high-bred client's offering good money. Join her as, with bungling incompetence, she follows a trail littered with missing antique teddies, hapless crooks, a misplaced Lord of the Realm, and dead bodies. Will Cass, and Scotland, survive?'

Even writing the blurb was fun as it had to give the impression of humour. This brings me to my first point with regards to why we should write humour – you can let your creativity really fly and discover depths you didn't even know you had. As this was a complete departure from my gritty police procedurals, I was understandably nervous. However, when reviews came in from

American reader saying this is a Scottish Stephanie Plum, I knew my experiment had paid off.

The above segues smoothly to my next point. Writing humour is a chance to experiment, to play around with words and develop different writing styles. Like all writing there are different forms and different sub-genres which you can consider. Whilst *Stephanie Plum* and *Cass Claymore* are over the top and in your face, other humour is more subtle. *Pride and Prejudice* by Jane Austen starts off with a genteel humour which sets the tone of the book.

'It is a truth universally acknowledged, that a single man in possession of a good fortune, must be in want of a wife.'

This is a more subtle type of humour which will resonate with different readers. You may be saying what's funny about that, yet to me it contains a humour which lets me know this is going to be a romance with a soupcon of humour to liven it up. Whatever your humorous tastes, you can bring it to your writing, and I will get into that in a moment.

I have mentioned sub genres so it would be useful to look at what these are to give you a more balanced view of whether you would like to write humour. Have you read in any of these genres, and do any of them resonate with you? That would be a natural starting point for your exploration of writing in the genre.
- Joke books
- Non-fiction

- Romantic comedy
- Cozy mystery
- Humorous mystery
- Science Fiction – think Hitchhikers Guide to the Galaxy
- Humorous fiction – P. G. Wodehouse
- Children's

As I said, it is possible to bring humour to your writing whatever the genre in which you write. My DI Shona McKenzie Mysteries, although gritty crime, have some measure of humour within them. She is always thinking of ways to kill her boss as he gets on her nerves. There are a couple of Russian thugs who turn up in book two and they are still tormenting her in book seven as they seem to slide off every charge she ever throws at them. She calls them different names every time she mentions them, such as the Kalashnikov Brothers or The Bobbsey Twins. She describes one of the Lawyers as having a chest you could do the ironing on. These are light touches which give the reader pause for breath and bring a bit of levity to what could be a grim book; after all they are about serial killers. Shona also uses humour as part of her leadership style, alongside a bit of sarcasm. Sarcasm is one area of humour that needs to be used lightly as readers may not connect with the character if they see them as being cruel.

You can also bring humour into your non-fiction books as I have done with my *Writing Matters* series. In *Motivation Matters* I have an exercise called *Your Having a Giraffe* where I encourage writers to spend time reading humorous books or watching humorous television programmes. This releases chemicals which helps to prepare the brain for greater creativity. I also use humorous phrases to get my point across. Non-fiction lends itself beautifully to humour as much as fiction does.

. . .

The only books I have seen little humour in are Scandi Noir all of which seem to be grim after grim. However, these are excellent books, and they work. I think adding humour to these would take away from the storyline.

I would be doing you a disfavour if I did not mention humorous memoir. This is ripe for humorous anecdotes because life is jam packed with humour and humorous occasions. One of my favourite books is *Miss, What Does Incomprehensible Mean?* by Fran Hill. Fran is a gifted storyteller and can see humour in every situation. I would advise you to read her book if you would like to know how to write a humorous book.

I will finish with a line I believe is the funniest I have ever read in a book.

"Do you think your baby Jesus would like a cuddle, Mrs Virgin?" asked a small sheep politely.
Debbie Young

This line shows what good humour should be – every word carefully crafted to ensure comic effect.

I hope I have enthused you to give writing books containing humour a try. One final tip – if you see or hear anything funny, write it down immediately. You never know when it will come in useful.

Author Bio

Wendy H. Jones is an award-winning, international bestselling author of fifteen books in five different series, covering readers from childhood to adulthood. These include adult crime, young adult mysteries, children's picture books, and non-fiction for writers. She is currently writing a historical fiction book, the first in a new series. In addition, she is a writing coach, editor, and CEO of *Authorpreneur Accelerator Academy* - a membership supporting authors on their writing and publishing journey - and runs *Scott and Lawson Publishing*. You can find out more at http://www.wendyhjones.com

14

WHY WRITE LOCAL FICTION?

ELIZABETH POWER

When I began to write stories focused on the area where I grew up, I had no idea what I was doing. I only knew I yearned to represent the culture, history, and voices of the people who were in my head because they'd been part of my life. It turns out this type of writing is called "local fiction." I'm lucky. It's a strong, natural connection that goes back to my earliest years. It flows. Let me tell you why I love writing local fiction and why I think you might want to consider it too.

I remember sitting on my grandmother's lap and listening to stories as late into the night as my young eyes would stay open. The voices around me would become fainter and fainter; the sounds of the night air would quiet as I drifted off. Then, the following day, I would wake up in my bed, having been carried down the path and tucked in.

Those summer nights were enchanting. Every family tale—myth, truth, and outright lies—would be recounted, embellished, and shared with great theater. There were stories about black racer snakes that would chase children, complete with grown men chasing my cousins and me around the yard as they told them, much to the other adults' delight. There were stories about cows whose legs were shorter on one side because they walked hillsides. And then there the hushed stories about infidelity, failed relationships, divorces, deaths, and mysterious murders. Stories about childbirth and the supernatural were women's tales reserved for the kitchen, where they could barely be heard over the clanging of pots and pans.

These were the voices of the rural Southern Appalachian Mountains of North Carolina in the United States, where I grew up as the fourth generation on family land. Over the years, I've spent a lot of time listening to people's stories. We've sat around kitchen tables, outdoor fireplaces, pools of water from oceans in distant lands, and restaurants and bars in many places. They rest like jewels in a collection in my 'writer's memory,' that place in my mind where I store up snippets and bits of dialogue, storylines, and characters.

The stories from local areas, regions, and cultures form a central core in my life. They hold the idiomatic expressions that sometimes vex readers. They contain the wisdom unique to a culture that others may need to ponder on. Sometimes people need to ask, "Now, what does that saying mean?" And I guarantee they'll remember the saying and its meaning because it brings up a story.

Here, let me show you what I mean.

'Living behind the face.' This is Japanese; there, it means 'show only a pleasant to neutral face, keep your emotions inside you'. When I read this, I remember trips to Japan to work, preceded by Zoom meetings where I had no idea how people felt about the conversation based on their faces. Every business meeting, if it could talk, has a story about this. So does every after-work gathering, the place where dropping one's mask is formalized.

'Don't let them see you sweat.' Used more broadly in the United States, this phrase means almost the same thing. It's an emphasis on keeping calm when times are tough. This phrase reminds me of approaching a major exam and knowing that part of the trick was to act confident, even when I felt terrified. I could tell at least a dozen stories about this, about 'faking it until you make it', and other variations.

'Better to have a face like a stone slab', is Appalachian, from my part of the United States. It refers to showing no emotion. The face that accompanies it is droll. I remember hearing my great aunts reinforce this as a method to keep men from behaving in an untoward manner. It was seen as a protective advantage to show no emotions.

'Keep calm and carry on' and 'keeping a stiff upper lip' are phrases from the United Kingdom. The first phrase comes from a British WWII poster intended to help Britons prepare for war while maintaining life. The second is a classic British perspective, meant to encourage fortitude during adversity without letting one's upper lip tremble in fear. One of my 'adopted' mothers was a British war bride who taught me these sayings. There are lots of stories about her life in pre-war London.

Each of these reflects the use of language particular to areas with unique linguistic patterns. These phrases are shorthand statements that help us comprehend how people try to protect themselves by not showing emotions.

In many cases, it may be that people may use feelings as a weapon against you if others see them. Or, perhaps, containing emotions keeps group cohesion and strength in place. The stoic front may be someone's best efforts at appearing to be mature.

When I gather with people with whom I share a common characteristic, say, the same faith tradition, work, interest, or condition, it's the same dynamic. As a group, we have a common vocabulary, a shared experience. We share stories that help make sense of our shared world. If I were to write about our group based on a shared trait, it might be considered a form of local fiction.

I can write academic, business, and self-help materials 'like nobody's business' - a local phrase that means I'm good at it and fast. They use different dialects based on standard English, freer from idioms and constructs that mark it as from a particular area. They require vocabulary and styles specific to the topic and sector. If I write an article for a peer-reviewed medical journal about trauma and adapt it for use in a mass media or trade publication, the language, style, and constructs differ. Codeswitching among these dialects is a helpful skill.

But my love? Local fiction, those stories that incorporate some of the language and culture unique to where I grew up or rise from characteristics unique to a group of people.

What makes writing local fiction so valuable? Why is it important for authors to consider it as a genre?

Local fiction authors write about life outside the centres of power in a particular area. This is geographically based local fiction. From a broader perspective, local fiction can focus on groups of people outside of the centres of power. This is group-based local fiction.

Remote, isolated areas, small insular villages, areas with strong cultural identification, and islands are likely settings for local fiction. They are less influenced by power centres in typical ways and have higher likelihoods of localized ways of being. For example, Grit Lit is the writing from the Southern United States about the Southern United States. Grit Lit authors include Eudora Welty, Fanny Flagg, Flannery O'Connor, and William Faulkner. At the same time, stories from the Western part of the United States are just "Western fiction."

In Scotland, Arthur Conan Doyle (*Sherlock Holmes*), J.M. Barrie (*Peter Pan*), Dorothy Dunnet (historical fiction), and Scottish crime novelists including Wendy H. Jones are authors of local fiction. Local fiction is celebrated by The Royal Society of Literature, too, with the Ondaatje Prize. This annual prize celebrates a work of fiction, non-fiction, or poetry that evokes the 'spirit of a place'.

Authors around the world write geographically based local fiction. They write from experience or believably from research. While some critics may claim that the authenticity of being from a place is invaluable, authors who are 'not from here' can create believability. Sensitive editing preserves the voice and the unique elements their local fiction contains.

Authors who are outside of mainstream centres of power also write local fiction. The meaning of "local" shifts from geography to group in this case. Women, people of colour, indigenous peoples, those who identify as queer, those with disabilities, the mad community, people who are deaf, and others whose groups are disenfranchised or oppressed also write group-based local fiction. Local in this case refers to the characteristic that is unique to them, the difference that others might judge as a defect. Groups have in-group patterns of speech and inside knowledge that only people in their group - or those adopted by their group - will understand.

Whether based on geography or group, local fiction is a powerful tool. It preserves knowledge of local ways and customs that might otherwise go undocumented, even though it is fiction. It carries the voice of the setting and the people, and ideally, you can hear that voice in your head as a reader.

Imagine reading local fiction about an area you've always known existed but never visited. While the fictional story needs tempering with facts for believability and authenticity, readers experience dialect, dialogue, customs, and ways that are specific to the setting that makes the book "local fiction."

Increasing mobility from place to place and increasing acceptance of different groups gives regional fiction another vital role. In a tiny town not too distant from my childhood home, the language in the streets among older people was a combination of Italian and French. It was a community of immigrants from Northern Italy. Remember that this is in the then-isolated Southern Appalachians, where an immigrant community of Italians fleeing religious persecution would be an anomaly. Now? The language in those same streets is English, Southern Appalachian, and versions of Spanish. The Patois - the local language - is confined to snippets in homes and among older families.

Regional fiction about the community and its history was the foundation for an outdoor theatre production. This drama has run for over 50 years, preserving a uniqueness erased through assimilation. Without local fiction preserving the story of the Waldensians, their history would be lost.

Those elements of geography or a group that make it unique are in customs, topography, dialect, foods, traditions, and folklore. They may share common or disparate beliefs, but this "local colour" defines them. As the world becomes more homogeneous, local colour is fading, and regional fiction preserves a record of it

Regional fiction preserves awareness of disenfranchised groups and remote areas for the future. It refuses to allow the literature of our times to reflect only the lives of mainstream cultures. It enriches the colourful landscape of literature that is always at risk of representing only mainstream voices.

What makes local fiction unique is also what should cause authors to consider it as a genre. What is unique to your world and your culture? Is your geography that of a lesser-known area? An island? A mountain range? An environmental focal point, like Chernobyl, Muir Woods, or a place where there is an ancient henge? Are there quirks and eccentricities normal based on where you were or are?

Are you a member of a group of which others are suspicious? Perhaps you have experience with incarceration, disability, or mental illness? A religious organization often misrepresented? Perhaps LGBTQI or a person who is neurodiverse? Descended from people who were indentured or enslaved? An immigrant? Different in some other way?

If you're either - different by geography or group - you have great potential for writing local fiction. A difference as "ordinary" as handedness can make for the basis of a good work of local fiction: what if there were an entire community of only left-handed folks? Could there be a murder committed in that community? What if the murderer was only acting like a left-handed person to avoid being identified? Or maybe it was someone who is right-handed? How might weapons or markings or use patterns help answer the questions?

Perhaps shoe wear shows a hint: left-handed people are more often right footed, so there is heavier wear on the toes of their right shoes from pushing back from chairs and from leading with their right foot. The cuffs of long-sleeved shirts and other items of clothing show handedness. Patterns of wear are evident when the wearer performs repetitive tasks in one location.

Suddenly this one distinctive characteristic opens up the scope and breadth of the story. Writers who develop local fiction based on either geography or group can engage creativity in a whole different way. For example, a story about a group of left-handed people instead of right-handed people has a different frame of reference. This frame is also different if the author is left-handed.

Identifying and using different lenses is normal to people and places outside of the centre of power. People who live outside of normative society switch among frames or code switch to fit in. Increasing the focus on these different lenses can expose previously hidden options.

This left-handed group—how might being left-handed cause them to separate and live as a formal community? What might be different about being left-handed outside and inside their private neighbourhood? How might this impact the arc of the story? What actions might it change?

Local fiction requires strong settings, characters, deliberate narration by the author, and storytelling. My local fiction plots focus on illustrating the ways and rituals of the community.

My characters adhere to old or odd ways (compared to the dominant culture) or specific characteristics unique to the region. I use the contrast between the old and unconventional ways and the outside world's ways, for example, describing how a character in Appalachia hunts for a lost glass eye. The setting for this work in progress is the more rural areas nearest my childhood home. The characters are two strong sisters, never married. Maggie, the eldest, has lost her glass eye. Ruthie is washing dishes in the kitchen. A key characteristic of women in this setting is that they are strong, plain-spoken (if not coarse), and direct. They do not have room for frivolity.

Here they are:

"Well, how would I know where your eye is? I don't wear it; I managed to keep my two eyes intact! And I am surely to the Lord ignorant of what happens in that rat's nest of yours you call a room." Ruthie, in the kitchen, tugged her gingham shirtwaist dress down. She smoothed her apron, tucked a sprig of curly grey hair behind her ear, and wheeled majestically around to face the sink. She looked out across the valley.

"You shut up, or I'll piss on your teeth. And I mean it!" Maggie fired back.

In the window, Ruthie could see Maggie's behind. The reflection was of two dried-up little butt cheeks pressing against her housecoat, poking up like the gaunt hips of Jesse Eller's tired old cow. She was doubled over and looked like the backend of some yogini's bad, bad, downward-facing dog pose. Presenting like a bitch in heat. Hmph.

Then Maggie was down on the floor as if in some expansive sun salute fashioned only as it could be in the hills. She'd never heard of yoga, could care less about saluting the sun except with the single-fingered salutation common to young folks and people who lived lower."

The reference to hills, the valley, and lower are code. They tell people from there where they are and toss a hint to people who aren't. People from there divide the population into low-land and high-land families. They're separated by 500 feet in elevation.

The description of the clothes and mannerisms comparing Maggie to a yogini is something only low-land and more contemporary readers might recognize.

The conflicted relationship makes room for jilted lovers, murder, and more, all centred around reveries at Maggie's funeral. The funeral has several local characteristics, including the contrast between earlier funereal customs and the ones observed at Maggie's homegoing.

People read local fiction to reconnect with their uniqueness, disappearing ways of being, and ways that liberate them from focusing only on normative culture.

I love writing local fiction because it allows me to create worlds about the place I grew up, the culture of my youth, and areas of my life that are unique. It preserves the voice and the vision of a subset of folks whose ways are disappearing. It helps me recognize that I have a place and a voice in this world. It demands that I master creativity in a whole different way and fuels my passion.

Author Bio

Elizabeth Power, M.Ed., is a sought-after speaker, writer, and educator in Nashville, TN. As a writer, she publishes in the non-profit, business, and medical sectors and personal development. Her local fiction stories circulate among friends and readers, who beg her to read them aloud and write more.

15

WHY WRITE HISTORICAL FICTION?

LORRAINE SMITH

You may never have considered writing historical fiction but join me as I share why I think it is a genre worth your consideration.

Historical fiction is a literary genre where the story takes place in the past. Historical novels attempt to capture the details of a specific time period as accurately as possible whilst the story itself remains fiction. Relevant details may include manners, customs, social norms and traditions. Looking at the small things which make up our social systems can be fascinating. What I have discovered really helps me as an author to bring the reader into a total experience of the time.

When checking what types of soaps were available at the turn of the century, I discovered that looking at newspapers from the time showing the advertisements gave me what I needed to bring authenticity to my story. We can see what the norms were for beauty, for instance Pears soap and Imperial Leather soap were popular. I am fascinated these soaps can still be found today. This gives my writing the authentic touches which take the reader back in time.

Many novels tell fictional stories that involve actual people and events. I am particularly interested in the period of the First World War and up to and including World War Two because I had two Grandfathers who served in WWI. Both were volunteers rather than conscripts. Bringing such personal stories into your writing gives it a richness and depth born from passion.

My paternal grandfather joined the Royal Scots Fusiliers in 1915 before my father was born and was killed in action in September 1915 when my father was five months old. As a child this made me sad. I could only know my grandfather through others who knew him. However, now I have researched his life and war service, I think I know him better.

My Maternal grandfather joined the Black Watch in Dundee in 1915 and survived the war. My Father then went on to serve in World War Two.

I was born quite late to my parents who were both born in 1915, with a twenty-seven-year age gap between myself and my surviving brother and sister. As a child I grew up aware of both wars and hearing the family stories about each grandparent. My Father had thought his father a fool for joining up. This stuck with me, and it was not until I decided that I wanted to find out about him and write his story that I found that many men in Dundee, and no doubt many other places, joined up to provide a future for their children.

The Separation Allowances paid during WWI were more than wages for most men. If they died, their wives and children were paid a pension. Men were selling themselves to the war machine for a future for their families. I believe these were brave men indeed. One lived and one died. Sad you might say, but both were brave and honourable men doing the best for their families and their country.

· · ·

Writing stories about such events allows us to understand what happened. Even after we have the facts we still search for sense and meaning. For me the research made sense of the senseless. The question my father could never answer - why my grandfather joined up was most probably for money and pensions for his sons. This guaranteed them a future.

The historical novelist exposes the reader to the inner lives of people across time and place and by doing this we can tell the untold stories, allowing the reader to experience the events through the eyes of those who lived through them. That is why I write, to bring my families' untold stories to life. I can also find the reason for why they acted as they did, and this can often surprise you.

The First World War was catastrophic in loss of life but also the loss of a way of life. Social upheaval created conditions for women to be more independent, campaign for the vote, and have careers of their own. These were changing times and writing about them in a fictionalised account can bring them into focus for many more people than in a factual account. It offers a more personal and intimate view when the story is about their own City and people they know.

The World is made up of ordinary people like you and me. Our parents and grandparents did their best as ordinary people in extraordinary circumstances. This has shaped and created our world as we know it today. I write about this period because it brings to life the people who lived here before me, gave me my values, and lived through world shaking events.

Historical fiction as we know it in contemporary Western Literature dates back to the early 19th Century. Leo Tolstoy, Sir Walter Scott, Honore de Balzac and Janes Fenimore Cooper were among the first Novelists to explore historical settings as a concept for a book, The genre was also popular in the United

States in the early 20th Century, where the focus was War stories, mostly the American Civil War.

I am passionate about doing this for Dundee and the people who lived or died through these times. One of the major elements of historical fiction has been an expression of national character and self-definition. There is no doubt that Dundee in World War One was a good example of how our national identity is formed. This war also gave us insight into the extremes of human behaviour, trench warfare, cruelty and the ability to withstand unthinkable conditions. Writing about this helps us retain the past and the vast catalogue of writing about the First World War in poetry, newsletter, diaries, memoir and letters have ensure that we have retained this era of our past. Writing about our past contributes to its longevity in memory.

If you want to write great historical fiction, then you have to add meat to the bones. You must be interested in your time period. The more I research and find out it feeds my passion to continue.

The intersection and blurring of fact and fiction help to define any historical novel. We all know what the famous characters in history accomplished because we can read about it in history books. However historical evidence is often partial and incomplete, and most historians include some element of interpretation. Your passion for the time period about which you are writing can help in building the world your characters live in. What foods are they eating or what does the town look like? The immediate surroundings. What are their clothes like? What do the houses look like? What books and music do they read and listen to? This can give the reader insight into the mind of a member of a past society which creates empathy and a live connection between them, then and now.

. . .

All this means research – I started by doing some simple family history. This led me down the rabbit hole of who my grandparents really were. Not just some young couple caught in a war but the reasons behind my grandfather volunteering for the Royal Scots. I found that he came from Ayr, where he was caught in a mining accident which killed his brother, my uncle. He came to Dundee and met my grandmother. The rest as they say is history. This is how they came alive for me I can see the places they saw. Quite literally walk in their shoes, to the parks and streets and places they knew.

This is where the journey begins, research opens up a whole new avenue. My father was never aware that my grandfather had survived a mining accident which killed hundreds. I found it by chance, on a hunch. While I can never be definite. I believe this was the reason for the move to Lochee. If there is another, I can never know, and this is where the fiction part of the narrative comes in.

This is also where fact meets speculation in order to provide a foundation for my story. The back story of his parents left behind in St Quivox, and the other real and fictional characters in the book are also a part of this foundation.

My book is set in Dundee in 1914. At that time Dundee was the jute capital of the world. This one city provided jute to the rest of the world. It was the home to the Jute Barons who monopolised the trade worldwide. My grandmother was a spinner and worked in Camperdown Works. This was a vast complex where jute was delivered raw from India, then 'scutched' - the softening process which made it ready for spinning into a workable fibre. The complex had its own railway to deliver processed jute between the different parts of the complex, horses also to pull carts. The small village of Lochee was home to over 50,000 workers mostly women and small children - shifters who cleared the jute dust from under the spinning machines. Those who staffed the mills and created vast wealth worked twelve-hour days. Children were half-timers who were schooled for a morning and then worked at the Mill. Into this mix came insanitary conditions, cholera, typhus and the social upheaval created by workless men. This is the world my characters inhabit. It will also dictate how they react and interact with each other and their larger social environment. Each world we create will have limits and restraints created by the social dictates of the era.

A novel differs from a history book because it recounts the factual touch points from the past through the telling of the character's story and how the character thinks and feels. Writing a novel whose backdrop, World War One, is so vast and well known, raises a concern that the historical facts and details have to ring true without overpowering the story. As a writer the challenge is to understand the concrete world that your characters live in and interact in.

Jerome de Groot in his book *The Historical Novel* states that Historical fiction offers an 'analysis of recognisable human character within a specific set of circumstances - so that we can re-experience the social and human motives which led men and women to think feel and act as they did in historical reality.'

As a child I grew up aware that my father had been in World War Two. I also knew that his father, my grandfather died in 1915, when my father was five months old. This defined my father in many ways and had a long and lasting effect on him and also my grandmother. This is why I am writing to tell their story and others here in Dundee.

War provides a vast array of material for a writer. These are situations that most of us fear, for ourselves and our sons and daughters. Those who experience war are often changed irreparably by what they experience. Also, those whose circumstances are defined by the effects of war.

Perhaps one of the best examples of this type of storytelling is film. The movie, Saving Private Ryan is a good example of real events involving the Normandy landings in 1944. the basis of the plot has some truth but most of the action is fictional and interwoven with the real facts of the time period. None of us can know what happened to each man but the story gives us a real emotional experience of what it was like.

My Father was a veteran of D Day, and he did not speak about it often; when he did, I used to wonder just what it had been like in reality. I could not imagine my dad capable of killing anyone. This was something my research quickly corrected. I had found a side to my father that perhaps in hindsight I wish I did not know.

Our inability to imagine things we have never experienced is limited and fraught with inaccuracies. I have a few family facts such as my paternal grandfather died at Ypres in 1915 and my maternal grandfather survived WWI. Like most families, their exploits in war were not known until after their deaths. The small snippets of information I remember from my childhood can be corroborated by research. The story is mine to write, fact and fiction interwoven to bring my family to life. My Father was an excellent example of a Primary Source. As he grew older, he was more willing to talk, and I wish I had written it down or recorded it. I can say that his recounting of D Day and his experience of war was just as dreadful as anything written since.

I want to bring them to life in my novels. I want to tell their stories. I can use these to build a world where a reader can immerse themselves in the time period, namely, Dundee in 1914.

I need to be accurate in the details. Social norms were quite different then, and Dundee upset the balance when women and children became the family breadwinners. Men were too expensive to employ. This created a social situation which involved a challenge to the traditional role of women as wives and mothers, leaving men jobless, at home, looking after children as 'Kettle Bilers'. This was only part of a social move which saw the rise of Trade Unions, Suffragettes, and the turmoil which led into WWI.

According to de Groot, 'the historical novel allows us to contemplate social change. We see the change in hindsight which allows the individual to reflect on their contemporary circumstances. It can also help us to trace the path of religious and political change.'

I see this as a reason to write historical fiction, my journey has been one of discovery and delight about family members I've known and those I have never known. we can bring the stories of the small people to life. World War Two has been described as the 'People's War'. Well, my family were those people, and yours too. Those who fought and those who stayed at home, and those who never came home.

By writing historical fiction I can educate people about the past, myself included. It can also serve as an expression of who we are and where we come from. It is part of our identity.

· · ·

Author Bio

Lorraine Smith is a native of Dundee. She writes historical fiction set between 1914 and 1945 and after. A Graduate of both Dundee University and University of Abertay. She now works as a civil servant.

Website: https://lorrainesmiith.pubsitepro.com

16

WHY WRITE ROMANCE?

WENDY H. JONES

Romance novels are generally regarded as being those where romantic love between two individuals is at the core of the book. Whilst this was traditionally between a man and a woman this has now expanded to include all romantic relationships, making it one of the most diverse genres in which to write. In addition, romantic novels are expected to have a satisfying ending which is considered optimistic regardless of the difficulties the main characters may face along the way. Whilst this could be seen as being one of the easier genres in which to write, any would be writer will find it is more challenging than first envisaged. However, the passion which ignites within you with regards to writing in this genre, can also be ignited within your characters – passion breeds passion as you write. Yes, I appreciate this could be somewhat confusing, but it is true.

So, why write romance? As humans we are all programmed to love and be loved an instinct we are born with. We are all searching for love and fulfilment in some way. Writing romance can be satisfying as when you do so you are bringing hope to the reader – hope that romance is possible, hope that they can find that romance, and hope that all will be well in the end.

Readers want to believe in a better world, and they want to be transported to a place they would like to be, with characters they would like to spend time with. Alongside hope, romance books also offer escapism, not only to the reader but to the writer who can escape into the romance that they are writing. They can be anywhere in the world, with anyone in the world, and be anyone they want to be. What a great way to make a living.

The romance genre is the number one best-selling genre in the world, regularly swapping places with the crime genre. When it comes to borrows in kindle unlimited romance tops the statistics year after year, and libraries cite romance and crime as being the most borrowed books. As I said previously, we write because we have passion burning inside us to write, but I also have a burning passion to pay my bills, eat, and travel around the world. So, I would suggest that money is an equally important factor in why we write. Passion comes in many guises – no wonder we need romance books for escapism.

There are numerous subgenres within the romance genre, meaning you, the writer, will never get bored. Here are some examples
- Sweet romance
- Romantic suspense
- Contemporary
- Historical
- Time travel
- Science fiction
- Religious
- Romantic comedy

. . .

These are just a few of the subgenres and each of these have their own subgenres. As you can see there is something for every writer to try their hand at. If you are not yet a writer, are any of these the type of book you like to read. If so, you will find your passion will come across in your writing. If you are an established writer, have you thought about expanding your offering to include suspense books in that genre. For example, if your passion is science fiction then you may wish to think about writing a series which combines both – not only will you find many of your existing readers will enjoy it, but you will pick up new readers. You will find there are many others passionate about your newfound love of writing romance books in your genre. As I write crime fiction, I am seriously considering writing romantic suspense; in fact, I am excited about the prospect. I have moved towards this as there is a bit more romance in my *Cass Claymore Investigates* series.

This leads me nicely on to why all authors should be writing romance. Romantic relationships should most often be one of the subplots within any book that you are writing. Consider what I said at the beginning of this chapter, we are all programmed to form relationships and we all long to be loved. Characters do not exist in isolation. I appreciate there are books where there are lone wolves but even in those there are relationships formed along the way. Whilst I do not write romance per se, my DI Shona McKenzie books contain a series arc around the romantic relationship between Shona and her love interest, Douglas Lawson, the procurator fiscal. There is also a measure of humour in here as often they meet each other at a crime scene. So, even gritty crime fiction can contain romance, a plot point which allows the reader to draw breath and relax slightly from the steadily rising tension. No man, or woman, is an island even in the grittiest of crime thrillers and to make them so would make them less relatable.

Romance writing and reading works because as humans we have a deep longing to be loved, accepted and to belong on a deep level. Writing romance taps into the visceral feelings we all have and allow us to explore them more deeply. When writing romance we can deal with our own questions, thoughts, and feelings, allowing us to express them in a way which is safe. Whether that book will be launched into the world is completely up to you. You may just write it to help you deal with your own situation or to see if you can do so, that is valid.

Conflict within romance books often comes from misunderstanding as does conflict within many other of the genres we have written. Real life and real relationships are packed full of misunderstanding making many situations fraught. The writer of romance can dig deep into their own experiences in order to bring this into play within the narrative. Drawing on life to create relationships, both simple and complex, can be one of the biggest joys of writing romance; it can also be one of the most challenging aspects. Drawing them to a close in a satisfactory manner, as is expected of the genre, is something which needs skill and attention to detail. This is true whether writing romance itself, or whether incorporating it into other genres.

Poetry also lends itself beautifully to the romance genre. Throughout history poets have been speaking of romance and penning poems to the ones they love. Consider William Wordsworth, John Keats, Percy Bysshe Shelley, and Robert Burns. The list is endless. Both Mary Shelley and Edgar Alan Poe were also romantic poets despite writing gothic and crime books respectively.

The sheer beauty of the language used in romantic poetry

cannot be underestimated. Take Burns A *Red, Red Rose* as an example:

'O my Luve is like a red, red rose
That's newly sprung in June;
O my Luve is like the melody
That's sweetly played in tune.'

The simple words of this poem have captured the hearts and minds of poetry lovers throughout the years and is still being recorded in song by contemporary artists. Yet, the poem also serves as a metaphor for the passing of time.

All Burns Poetry could be considered romance due to the use of the poetic language and the themes which he encompasses. Burns saw romance in every situation as can be seen in his poem *To a Mouse*.

'But Mousie, thou art no thy-lane,
In proving foresight may be vain:
The best laid schemes o' Mice an' Men
gang aft agley,
An' lea'e us nought but grief an' pain
for promis'd joy!'

Burns, a farmer, wrote this after he upset a mouse's nest whilst ploughing the fields. Through his words he got straight to the pain that the mouse must have felt at the destruction of his dwelling. The verse also gave birth to a well-known Scottish phase which is often used today. 'The best laid schemes of mice and men gang aft agley'.

. . .

In romance books, characters are key as the plot is mostly character driven. It is important to show them warts and all, their good points, bad points, flaws, and insecurities. These make the characters relatable. They also have to grow and develop, whilst surprising the reader. You are probably seeing from this that writing romance is not simple; it is challenging and exciting, it can bring your characters alive and give them a natural depth which readers will be attracted to, and it can allow them to show who they really are.

Romance, at its core, deals with human emotion. To portray that emotion in written form and elicit the corresponding emotion in your readers takes great knowledge, great passion, and great skill. The romance writer must use words which ignite the part of the brain which deals with emotion. When they do so they can bring the readers to tears, fill them with joy and elation, allow them to slow down and speed up and literally has the readers heart pumping. This comes with great responsibility, and I admire writers who take on that responsibility. I know when I write romantic scenes in my own works of fiction, they can be the most complex scenes to write. I want the reader to feel what I feel as I pour those feelings into my characters. This means the correct word choice is crucial. Yet, knowing I have chosen the correct word is exhilarating; it is a feeling like no other.

I believe we are all romantic at heart and that we can use that romance to write believable characters with stories which will capture readers hearts. I love writing the romantic arc to my fiction books and seeing how this helps my characters grow and become more rounded and more believable in the process. I would challenge you to try writing romance and can promise you, you will also be surprised. You never know where it might end.

Author Bio

Wendy H. Jones is an award-winning, international best-selling author of fifteen books in five different series, covering readers from childhood to adulthood. These include adult crime, young adult mysteries, children's picture books, and non-fiction for writers. She is currently writing a historical fiction book, the first in a new series. In addition, she is a writing coach, editor, and CEO of *Authorpreneur Accelerator Academy* - a membership supporting authors on their writing and publishing journey - and runs *Scott and Lawson Publishing*. You can find out more at http://www.wendyhjones.com

17

WHY WRITE BOOKS SET IN A DIFFERENT WORLD?

MARESSA MORTIMER

When it comes to writing books set in a different world, *Lord of the Rings* immediately springs to mind as being one of the best examples one can read. Yet, I only read the first book of *Lord of the Rings*, then gave up. Why? The book contains some amazing descriptions, and you can picture the mountains and paths quite easily. I loved his characters and how different the world looked. When it comes to world building, Tolkien was a master builder, and I did like it for that reason.

You might wonder, why should you write a book in an imaginary world? Many books are set in a fictional setting, even though they might be loosely based on existing places. Historical fiction requires a lot of research if you want to use a real-world setting, but you can still recognise these places and even visit them. It is lovely to recognise places and streets, or even people when you're reading. So why make up a completely fictional world?

I based my first book in Crete, using a setting I knew, and changing it slightly. I enjoyed it, as it transported me back in my mind. The amount of research needed was limited, as I could picture the setting easily. Then I learned about World Building, and a new world opened up for me. Literally. Building your world is such a powerful thing to do, for so many different reasons. I encourage you to try it for yourself.

It's not impossible, and if you have limited time, make sure you limit your world, as it's a real time-eater once you start! Tolkien spent a very long time on building Middle earth etc, and as the books demonstrate, it was all incredibly involved. This may be one of the reasons I did not continue, the sheer complexity overawed me. You might want to start more simply, and it will still be enjoyable. There are many podcasts and books about how to build a fictional world but looking around you when walking in a quiet forest or driving along winding roads, you might wonder why you should come up with something fictional. These are my reasons for enjoying world building, and why I loved building Elabi, as well as some other fictional worlds, in my mind.

It allows you to add all the things you like

When you write a book set in a certain town, it comes with limits. Writing about Cheltenham means that it would be hard to include an underground railway, as you will get inundated with letters and reviews, calling you out. No publisher will look at your handiwork, as there are no underground railways in Cheltenham. What if you insist on having an underground? Make your own town. I love manned lighthouses; coracles are the most intriguing little boats and I'm in awe of the military being able to move at speed with a heavy rucksack called a Bergen. The high-speed walk is called tabbing. Now, all those things should be in a book, preferably together. So, my first chapter of *Walled City* includes all these. With one publisher informing me they're all different timed items. I know. I made up this City-State Elabi because I wanted a world that would include all my favourite things.

I didn't start there, but once you build your world, it's so much fun adding the smaller details, and you will enjoy shaping the world you're building the way you want it. Writing is a wonderful activity. Writing and enjoying it is even better. So why not add the things that make you smile? Short stories are great for this kind of thing, as you can then grow them into full-length novels once you've figured out your world.

This is also true for fantasy. Why not have special chairs that pour out coffee and keep up your cake supply? You could invent things you would like. If your world has a historical feel, you might enjoy adding some bits of history in. That way, you get to keep the best of both worlds. If you have a family heirloom, you could spin an incredible story around this. In that case, your self-made world is not the focus, just a vehicle for an intriguing story.

It is great for trying out effects

If your world is fictional, you can try out ideologies and see what happens. You can try out new weapons and discover who might grab power. In a real setting, you would be limited. "The government would never allow that," would be an instant comment. Also, why would you get all your characters to sleep in tents with only one bathroom block for 2,000 inhabitants if Milton Keynes is just down the road?

In my Elabi Chronicles, I wanted to see what happened if you had a society where belief and emotion were banned. I had many interesting hours, watching my characters struggle with the Council and co-workers ready to betray them. It is also great if in your story you would like to blow up the local hairdresser. With just one hairdresser in the village, that could cause dirty looks once locals read your book. If you're into chemistry, this is your chance to invent that special potion or powerful substance. You can try out ideologies without losing your membership to your local political party.

Having another world as your setting gives you the chance to look at characters a lot. You can have different social structures. When you can do with your world what you like, it can help to make societal structures clearer. By making your world larger than life, it can spread out problems, making them more visible or less of a problem. It also involves a different kind of research. My area in Elabi that is called Beyond the Hills isn't nice at all. Although various regimes have held similar re-education facilities, it would involve a lot of research, some of which would be out of date already, hard to access or tricky when it comes to copyright. Beyond the Hills, I was in charge, and I could make the poor inhabitants struggle in whatever way I deemed fit. Would they try to escape? And how would I keep them usefully employed?

You can change limits

Most books are bound by limits. You can play around with that a little, but people are quick to spot inconsistencies - "Steam trains hadn't been used for five years by then." I'm not keen on details, so if I used any maths or physics in my books, I would be in trouble. In a fictional world, the sky is the limit, and even that is not limited. In college, we were introduced to The Land of Oct. This is a Dutch maths activity, where you work in 8s. So, number nine was actually eleven. As I said, Maths is not my thing, so the Land of Oct was not a destination I would ever choose for a holiday. If you enjoy that kind of thing, your new world would be the perfect place to try it out. Just make sure you choose an editor that likes maths as well.

Of course, if you do any kind of writing with children, this is an excellent exercise for them to do. They can 'do what they like' as long as it still makes sense in their world. It will allow them to answer all their 'What If' questions. Also, the change of limits can help you to rewrite history. That boyfriend in Year

One who refused your proffered sweets? Well, here is your chance to change the outcome. When writing about something that could be painful, the fact that it is set in another world gives you that extra step away from it, making it easier to process the feelings involved. The same goes for people reading your stories. It's easier to allow yourself to get drawn into a fictional world than to imagine a hairdresser being blown up in Painswick.

It's a great way to use your imagination

Making up your world is the perfect way to allow your imagination free reign. Fantasy books are often in made-up worlds. It allows for dragons, elves, walking trees or anything else that takes your fancy. Maybe you want to invent a whole new species. This would be so much fun to do. You sit down and write, draw or type your new place and people. Any person can have five heads. This might cause problems later in your story, but it will also allow you to think through the details. One of the good things about writing in a different world is that you can enjoy thinking about it. You might need a lot of time before the story starts to simply think about the place and imagine yourself there.

It allows you to think about other languages, diets, religions and festivals. It's not just a matter of writing, "Once upon a time, there was..." but you will need to think through the details. It is a great way to help you to visualise your story and characters and will also help you to live in the moment with your characters. Everything has to be thought about, and you will find that once you start, it will be hard to stop. It makes you look at the world around you as well. Why do people do the things they do? Will you keep it in your world, or are you going to change people's attitude to contact lenses or sandals?

With my children, I often find allowing their imagination to go wild helps them to come up with a better story. If it has to fit into a known setting with predictable characters, they struggle. It's hard to let your imagination go if all you have to do is look around you to see what is there. It slows you down from being creative and it can make your dialogue stilted. However, if there is an Elves Convention, and two Elves turned out to be part of a large pickpocketing ring, think of the commotion that would bring.

There is scope for new names

I love names, especially if they have a meaning. This is one of the things I love the most about plotting my books: coming up with names for the characters. For my *Elabi Chronicles*, I used Latin words, then twisted them into names. This allowed me to choose names that told me about the person. Some of the fantasy books or books set in other cultures make it hard to remember names. I don't often look at names too closely when reading, which works as long as the names aren't too similar. What kind of names do you want characters to have? Again, you can use your imagination and simply enjoy coming up with names. One of the things I have found with "real" names, I always check that there isn't someone already walking around with exactly that name. You wouldn't want a CEO of some large company mixed up with tales of mayhem and murder.

Maps and worlds

I can't draw to save my life, so to see gorgeous hand-drawn maps can make me feel a tad green-eyed. I do use maps though, and again, there are websites and programmes where you can design maps. For me, it's the freedom to design a city or country in whatever way I want. Want a river? Have two! Of course, your map needs to make sense, but there is a real thrill in drawing new lands. Will it be the southern or northern hemisphere? What kind of climate? I knew nothing about the southern hemisphere, apart from the idea that they celebrate Christmas on the beach. So Elabi is based in the southern hemisphere, and my editor helped me with the timings of snow and sun. It is great to see a new island take shape. It is part of allowing your imagination to picture things. Drawing a road along the coastline of your new land: what kind of views do you get? Will the road be hot and dusty, or are your characters glad when the wind is blocked by some trees?

Making maps helps you to get deeper into your story. It gives your characters a setting you can picture. It helps to keep the story straight as well: was their house to the left or right of the shop? Having a map helps to see the steps your character needs to take to escape before the dragon finds out his favourite diamond has gone missing. It tells you the tools your characters need: scaling a cliff with a huge diamond under your arm is going to be hard work, so you might have to rethink that bit. I recently reviewed a fantasy novel, *Of Fire and Blood*. You know one of my favourite things in the book? He had added drawings of some of the main characters as well as a detailed map. I loved looking at the beautiful, pencilled drawings, and it helped me, as a reader, to engage with the story even more.

Those are my reasons for World Building. Of course, there is nothing wrong with setting a story in Hull or Folkestone. But I would recommend giving World Building a try. Why? Because it makes you look at the world around you in a new way as well. You will be more aware of details in life. Apart from anything else, the freedom and imagination that will be yours when building a new world will bless you in many ways. I hope you'll give it a try as I have found it gives me so much joy, and I love to see other people find this way to release their creativity as well.

Author Bio

I grew up in the Netherlands and moved to England soon after finishing my teaching training college. Married to Pastor Richard Mortimer we live in a Cotswold village with our four children. I'm a homeschool mum, enjoying the time spent with the family, travelling, reading, and turning life into stories. I want to use my stories to show practical Christian living in a fallen world. You can find out more at:

https://vicarioushome.com

18

WHY WRITE POETRY?

KIRSTEN BETT

When I tell people I love writing poetry, they look at me in awe. I don't know why, I have had only a few poems published. They often add: "Oh, that is so hard." But it's not. If you love words, you'll love poetry. If you like writing, you'll like writing poetry. It's a bit like dreaming words. I hope you'll dream along with me.

My love of poetry started young, it was inspired by a poem that spoke to me, about shadows. It was a fun day. Picture this: two kiwi kids of about seven years old. OK, they might have been eight. They were reciting a poem. Kim knew it by heart, I didn't. We were on the grass of Murray's Bay Primary, lying on our backs staring at one of those iconic New Zealand blue skies; a few white clouds were passing. We were guessing what they resembled while reciting this poem. It could have been *A Shadow* by Robert Louis Stevenson because that was published in The Golden Book of Poetry in 1947, and our clouds were going by at the end of the sixties.

When I got home I could not remember the poem exactly so I created my own. The first two lines have always stayed in my mind:

My shadow always follows me On the beach and into the sea
They pretty much sum up my life at the age of seven. You'd come home from school and go to the beach. I gifted my first poem to Mrs Hutchinson the next day. She made a song and dance about how the poem was written by someone else. But after looking up the famous poem, she got back to me with apologies. Only to kindly direct me to the playground for a lesson in drawing shadows. I looked and looked at my illustration and thought it was sheer perfection. But she stood beside me and said: "Look at your own shadow, where does it start?" Aha, apparently not as a separate entity...

Illustrating aside, this is where my passion for poetry came from. My kiwi friend Kim grew up to become a poet and musician. At the age of 10, my family took me to the Netherlands where I had to learn Dutch and forgot about writing poetry. Towards the end of the eighties, Kim sent her friend, poet, David Eggleton, who was performing at Poetry International in Rotterdam to do a reading at my neighbourhood pub. I had bought his book *South Pacific Sunrise* and was blown away by his performance that was full of life and rant. At school poetry was the most boring topic, but Eggleton's poetry was on fire. He is, at the time of writing, the New Zealand poet laureate until August 2022. When my friends and he had a drink afterwards, he implied I had something of a poet in me. Maybe I just thought he said that, maybe it was the beer talking. I didn't care, I dusted my pen, and my love affair with poetry was rekindled.

Yet, it wasn't until I was back in New Zealand about two decades later that I started my online Diploma in Creative Writing at Polytechnic Whitireia. The most important thing I discovered was that although I had gained an excellent command of Dutch, English is my language for creative writing. That was a vital eye-opener. So, if you are bilingual as well, try writing a poem in your first language, see where it takes you.

A bit of magic

Training can give your poetry a kick-start but workshops, and competition, keep the fire going. I took the IOWA Poetry Workshop at the University of Wellington and participated in a workshop in the Wairarapa from the Australian poet Alan Jefferies. He gave me confidence to keep on writing poetry. While honing your craft is important, some writing groups can be unjustly critical. I had experienced that and almost closed that chapter. Thanks to Alan and the participants of his workshop, I kept on going.

You do need deadlines and constructive feedback to kindle the fire though. Finding the right writing group is critical. For me in recent years that has been the online, international workshops by the Irish poet Kevin Higgins. He provides a very respectful and stimulating environment that I highly recommend. He usually starts workshops for the period of three months. Google Kevin Higgins online workshops for more information.

Workshops are great for working on poems but there is a bit of magic involved in getting the poem itself going. As mentioned, for me it's almost like dreaming. My poems usually come to me in the middle of the night. So it could be that I am thinking about an assignment before I go to sleep. Maybe I will awake with a few lines. This can also happen if something has happened in the day that had a great impact.

At the end of May this year, a few lines appeared as I was brutally woken up by the crows' early morning. They sleep in a nearby park on a tree and a few birds always land on our roof after the crowd has taken off. I don't know why. I normally hear them, think some swear words, and go back to sleep. But this particular morning, they inspired a poem. I wrote down a draft straight away. Here's the edited version:

Wake-up call

While his crowness disposes
his shit on the loungers below,
screeches, roof taps, 5 am
call but a short flight
from his sleeping tree.

Another roof comes to mind
al fresco coastal dining,
backdrop's a gull killing
a different kind's nestling.
Pet Cemetery at a wedding.
We would never be that cruel.

It was a few days after the plane carrying Raman Pratasevich and his girlfriend Sofia Sapega had been 'hijacked' in Russia. That was not on my mind when I wrote the lines about the crows but the event crept in. It must have been bugging me unconsciously. I love that poetry can help you process this crazy world. Even if the outcome is not 'happily ever after' it is worthwhile to know what is on your mind. I find that a notepad and a pen, or a note app on your phone, are great to have nearby. Just jot down words that come to you, don't overthink it and you have the beginnings of a poem.

Read a poem that grabs you

A passion for writing poetry comes with a passion for reading poetry. You just need to find a poem that grabs you. It's not hard. Poems are all around us. Where I live, they are carved into tablets on the streets. If I skim the lines of a poem I see on the street, in a window, on a wall and it hits me, I like to read it closely. Mostly I take a picture of the poem and read it at home, line by line. To see the connections and the juxtapositions. To wonder if the poem is really about birds or maybe it says more about us. The beauty of poems is that they can mean different things to different people. That is what is supposed to happen. Unlike what you might have been told at school, there are no rights or wrongs. As soon as you read the poem, you're in charge. Within reason, within the context – the time and the setting -- of the poem.

One of my favourite poets is Emily Dickinson (1830-1886), mostly because she was ahead of her times, didn't care about conventions or traditions but wrote beautiful poems that could also be critical of the society she lived in. Her language is stunning, and very easy to read. Yes, the two can go together. If you are new to poetry, she is a good place to start.

Clive James (1939 -2019) is another of my favourites. He has written a great poem *Dreams Before Sleeping*. It's in his Collected Poems. I like it so much because it describes how when you try and make yourself go to sleep, you just go round in circles. The paths the mind takes in doing so are funny and recognisable. They sometimes lead to brilliant poems like this one.

Podcasts on poetry

If you now feel inclined to set your inner poet free, a good next step could be to listening to podcasts on poetry. I recall one fabulous podcast with Alice Walker on Desert Island Discs.

Just look for their archive online. She spoke so softly, yet every word held weight. It inspired me to write a poem about her.

The New Yorker Poetry monthly podcast is another favourite. I dug into their online archives to prepare for this chapter. The December 2020 podcast caught my eye. It featured Margaret Atwood who is in her eighties now and has a wealth of insights to share. The format of this podcast is that the guest poet choses a poem that has been published in the New Yorker. The guest poet reads this poem out loud – a treat in itself -- and then discusses it with The New Yorker Poetry Editor Kevin Young. The guest poet then reads out a poem of themselves and that gets discussed as well. The podcast lasts about half an hour.

The poem Atwood and Young discussed first was A Stranger by Saeed Jones, followed by her own poem *Flatline*. Please listen to the podcast if you want to hear the poems. What I took away for this chapter were pearls of wisdom. Both poems had death as their theme. Atwood's partner of many years died of an illness they knew would kill him. Her latest collection *Dearly* contains the poem *Flatline*. The end is especially brilliant, but I won't spoil it for you. Atwood said, "Poetry is a way of coming to terms with things you don't wish to happen but know they will."

Atwood started her writing career as a poet because it merged better with her day job. She explains the difference between novel writing and poetry writing: "Writing a novel is work. One part inspiration, nine parts perspiration is what they say." She goes on to say that when a poet is working, nobody recognises it as work. They only see a person in a café, walking, staring out a window. "The difference between poetry and a novel is you can't summon a poem, you can put yourself in the zone, but you can't snap your fingers and say, you know... If you are stuck, you have to go to sleep or go for a walk."

Young agrees. "The unconscious needs to be there."

.   .   .

Rhyme to remember

Atwood writes all her poems longhand, Young confesses he writes on his phone. But poetry started off before writing existed. Putting text to rhyme or music helped people remember certain events, law, genealogy, and folklore. Often poems were more like songs, hymns, or chants.

Spoken poetry has never been away, because poets and writers have never stopped giving readings of their work. But since a few years performance and slam poetry has made a come-back. Kae Tempest was one of the first performance poets I heard; her energy and word speed on stage are mind-boggling. Slam poetry follows its own set of rules and, again, there is a lot of information and training online.

In the past, poems had to follow strict instructions according to their poetic form, for example a sonnet or a limerick. You no longer have to follow a form as long as it has rhythm and flows. But I still love experimenting with certain structures. The prescribed repetition of words or rhyme help me focus and make writing poetry almost like solving a sudoku. It's especially entertaining if you chose words that can mean different things for the repeating lines or words, because their new context in the poem will bring completely new, often humorous dimensions.

Haikus are the most compact form of poetry, I think, and apparently the most popular form. They are only made up of 17 syllables in three lines of 5 – 7 – 5 syllables and traditionally they need to bring some form of sudden enlightenment or illumination. There are lots of haiku competitions about.

Modern poetry still has to adhere to certain rules regarding the use of words, the vibrancy of the poem, or the economy of language, to name a few. But you know what? If something bad has happened to you and you want to throw a stone through a window, throw that stone through your pen on a piece of paper. Who cares what the rules are? If you want to show it to the outside world later, you can always come back to chip away until your diamond shines. That is what I most like about poetry, and I hope having read this you are keen to give it a go.

Author Bio

Kirsten Bett now lives in the Netherlands, but she has also lived in New Zealand for large parts of her life. Her partner Wim and she have downsized their life, so they have time to do what they love. Kirsten loves writing. She studied creative writing at Whitireia Polytechnic in New Zealand and is publishing her first book in 2021. You can read more about her work on her website: kirstenbettauthor.com

19

WHY WRITE NON-FICTION?

WENDY H. JONES

Many of the genres contained in this book fall within fiction or lend themselves more readily to fiction. However, I would be doing you an injustice if I did not cover non-fiction as part of the creative offering. Non-fiction lends itself to just as much creativity as fiction. In fact, it could be argued that more creativity is required to produce compelling non-fiction. You may find these statements astonishing; you may believe that non-fiction is merely musty old tomes that no one would want to read. If you do, you would not be alone. The reality is, non-fiction, especially narrative non-fiction, can bring a subject to life, allowing the reader insight into a topic they had never previously considered, and can do so in fresh and vibrant ways.

Just like any genre, the starting point for writing non-fiction is born from passion, usually a passion around the subject matter about which you are writing. Or that passion may be to prove to yourself that you can do something different. Whilst most writers know their non-fiction subject matter intimately, others have started with a general interest, researched the topic, and have written a book. Passion certainly helps but there are numerous books written by those who write to market when a subject is a hot topic. Recent examples are the COVID pandemic or climate change. It is possible to write a non-fiction book by researching the topic and delivering your own unique spin. If you are saying, I don't know enough about that, I would like to challenge you - by thoroughly researching the topic you will ultimately know more than many of the people who read your book. Focussing down on a niche can also help; you will find your passion in the process.

Creativity Matters was born from passion and desire - my passion for writing and my desire to share that passion with others. More prosaically, I also wanted to give other writers a platform to share the passion for their genre. Ultimately, I wanted to ignite a passion in you, the reader.

Non-fiction encompasses every single genre mentioned in this book and can be equally as creative. I would like you to do the following exercise. For each of the genres below I have given one example of a non-fiction book which could stem from that genre. I would like you to come up with one example for each using your own interests and passion. You never know it may be the seed that grows a book and lead to publication. Taking bold steps such as this gives your creativity wings.

Crime
A history of London in 20 crimes.
Humorous
You've got to laugh: the funny side of a writer's life
History

A biography of Scottish writers.

Whisky and Crime Fiction: The perfect combination

Science Fiction

What on earth, or beyond, is science fiction and where will it take us?

Romance

The greatest romances of our time.

Children's Books

Harnessing a child's imagination and creativity.

These are just off the top of my head, and I don't write in most of these genres, but they give an idea of what can be done. I am sure you will come up with many more all of which will be infinitely better than my attempts. This exercise will feed your creativity and one of the ideas you generate may spark a burning desire within you to write that book. As has been said, this is not a how to book but it does allow you to explore ways in which you can expand your own creativity whether writing fiction or non-fiction.

Like its fiction counterpart non-fiction can also be broken into sub-categories – manuals, how to books, historical, and guides amongst many others. One such sub-genre is narrative non-fiction. What exactly is this? Let us begin by breaking this down into its separate parts. Narrative means story. Non-fiction means it is true or factual. So, together, narrative non-fiction means facts or truth presented as a story. There can also be some weaving of fact and fiction where the story is fiction but firmly rooted in fact. I am currently writing a fictionalised account of the life story of a young man called Thomas Graham who hailed from Ecclefechan and sailed the seven seas upon joining the Royal Navy. While everything about Thomas will be true, and the historical facts will be correct, the narrative will be fictionalised whilst maintaining as much truth as possible. This raises a moral dilemma where creative license is used to drive the narrative and some of what is written may not have happened. This moral dilemma can be interpreted differently by the individual author. I believe this is part of the challenge of writing narrative non-fiction and can be what makes it so interesting to write – producing a story which is enjoyable to readers and yet still holds true to the established facts. However, I believe I have a moral duty to inform the reader of this and let them make an informed choice as to whether to read it.

One of the masters of narrative non-fiction is Edward Rutherford who writes novels detailing the history of a country or area. I am currently reading *China*, but he also written *Sarum*, *London* and *Ruska*. Whilst he does very clearly say these are novels, they are steeped in historical fact, bringing the subject matter to life. If you would like to explore writing narrative non-fiction, I would advise you to read one, or all, of his books. Books such as this allow you the creative freedom to write great prose that will touch readers' hearts, whilst informing and educating on a particular subject. How can one do this? Let us look at the opening two lines to *China*.

'At first he did not hear the voice behind him. The red sun was glaring in his face as he rode across the centre of the world.'
Edward Rutherford.

Not only is this beautiful writing but it is slap bang into the middle of a fact, presented in narrative form. During the Qing Dynasty, China considered itself the centre of the world. The challenge of inserting facts such as this whilst sweeping the reader along in a story is what makes writing narrative non-fiction both interesting and exhilarating.

Another outstanding example of narrative non-fiction is *The Silk Roads: A New History of the World* by Peter Frankopan. There is no fiction in this book, yet the facts are presented in such a way that it reads like a story. I would highly recommend you read this as it may spark ideas as to the type of narrative non-fiction book you may wish to write.

Writing non-fiction can also be fun. Consider the *Horrible History* series which puts forward facts in a way which is readable, fascinating, and educational. This type of writing allows the author to explore every aspect of creativity as illustrations are presented alongside the facts and the narrative.

Non-fiction lends itself to the use of a rich variety of language in all its different forms to bring the facts alive and have them leap of the page and into the reader's conscious mind. Anyone thinking of writing in this genre is in for a pleasant surprise. They, themselves, will be caught up in the sheer joy of the richness of the genre where they bring their passion for their topic alive. The excitement of opening up that topic to new readers and new converts is indescribable.

One may also write a non-fiction book to pass on knowledge and to help others. My non-fiction offerings are part of my *Writing Matters* series. This is the third book in the series with the first two being, *Motivation Matters* and *Marketing Matters*. I wrote these because I saw others struggling with both motivation and marketing and I wanted to produce tools that would help them. Although these are how to books and full of facts that will help other writers, they are also written in a light-hearted style. I was able to play with words and ideas to bring a book which would both inform and entertain, which could be both educational and fun. This balancing act gave me an opportunity to look at different ways in which to get the information across. I loved this challenge and enjoyed every moment. Here's an example from *Motivation Matters*.

'If your brain is telling you you can't draw, tell it to get stuffed.'
Wendy H. Jones

Now, how often do you hear that in a book. This exercise was designed to allow writers to explore different aspects of their creativity and expand the use of all parts of their brain. The premise being discussed is that your brain will believe whatever you tell it to believe. So, if it says you can't draw, it's time to tell it otherwise. Saying all of this makes sense and yet the sentence above says it more directly. It was also a barrel load of fun. Yes, writing non-fiction can be fun which is where I started this chapter.

I've also had fun writing this chapter. I am constantly full of wonder knowing that people enjoy my non-fiction books and that they find them helpful. This is a privilege – a privilege that you too can know if you decide to follow the non-fiction route. I hope I have inspired you to at least consider it and my wish for you is that you will enjoy it as much as I do. It's time to step out of your comfort zone and share the passion inside you.

Author Bio

Wendy H. Jones is an award-winning, international bestselling author of fifteen books in five different series, covering readers from childhood to adulthood. These include adult crime, young adult mysteries, children's picture books, and non-fiction for writers. She is currently writing a historical fiction book, the first in a new series. In addition, she is a writing coach, editor, and CEO of *Authorpreneur Accelerator Academy* - a membership supporting authors on their writing and publishing journey - and runs *Scott and Lawson Publishing*. You can find out more at http://www.wendyhjones.com

20

WHAT NOW?

This is now your time. Whether you are starting your journey as a writer, or whether you are an established writer, I would strongly encourage you to explore writing in each of these genres. Some may resonate with you more than others. If that is the case, then start with those that excite you the most. Jot down the genres that you felt tugging at your creative heartstrings. The ones where an idea is fluttering at the edge of your brain. Jot these down in a notebook and allow them to grow and develop. Before you know it, you will be writing stories that you had never previously considered. Or you will be adding elements to your existing fiction which will give it added zing and allow it to leap from the page.

It may be that you want to try your hand at flash fiction. If that is the case, then why not try writing a flash fiction piece in each of the genres in this book. I know I intend doing that as it will help me to develop as a writer and push the boundaries of what I can achieve. Whether these are ever used is another matter, but I believe that these will help me to develop as a writer and my existing work will be all the better because I have done so.

Is there a competition you would like to enter but the genre is one with which you are unfamiliar? Have you caught the passion for trying something in that genre? Be bold and put pen to paper. You never know what you will be able to achieve unless you try.

Fortune favours the brave and the future belongs to those who are not afraid to step out. This is your time, grab it with both hands on the keyboard, or one hand clutching a pen. It is then that magic will happen.

21

AND FINALLY

The purpose of this book was to allow you, the reader, to discover your creativity and develop a passion for writing in different genres. It is now over to you to explore each of these genres further. You may find that some resonated more than others, but I am confident your brain will now be buzzing with ideas.

At this point you may be wondering where on earth do I start? The answer is simple - by picking up a notepad and pen or opening your computer and a word processing document. Jot down ideas. Jot down which of the genres resonate with you the most. From those germs of ideas stories will grow.

Now that you have found your passion for writing, or at least a spark, help to make that passion grow. I would also encourage you to join a writers' group whether a physical group or an online group. The Scottish Association of Writers, of which I am President at the time of writing, has numerous affiliated groups which you can join if you are in Scotland. You can find more information on their website. There are also online courses you can take which will help you with your journey. I run several courses and you can find these on my website wendyhjones.com/courses.

I can think of no better way to finish this book than with the following words:

'The future belongs to those who have the courage to believe in the beauty of their dreams.'

Anon

It is now time for you to spread your wings and follow your dreams. I wish you all the best with your writing journey; it's the most exhilarating journey in the world.

REFERENCES

Introduction
Pamuk, Orhan (2011) *The New Life*, Faber and faber

Chapter 1
Eco, Umberto (1996), *The island of the Day Before*: Vintage
Morrison, Toni (2015) in *The Handy English Grammar Answer Book* by Christine A. Hult: Visible Ink Press
Vonnegut, Kurt (2010) *Palm Sunday: An Autobiographical Collage*, Vintage Digital

Chapter 6
Margetts, Joy (2021) *The Healing*, Instant Apostle

Chapter 8
Walls, Jeanette, (2021) quoted in 5 Reasons to Write Your Memoir, Writing Though Life (Quoted from Writers Digest) Online [Accessed August 2021]

Chapter 9
Flood, Alison (2020) *Crime fiction boom as book sales rocket past*

2019 levels. Guardian Newspaper Online, 7 July 2020 [Accessed August 2021]

Jericho Writers (2021) *Tips for Writing Crime Fiction and Thrillers*, Online, [Accessed August 2021]

Pound, Ezra (1968) *ABC of Reading*, Faber

Chapter 11

Morrison, Toni (1981) spoke at the annual meeting of the Ohio Arts Council and *The Cincinnati Enquirer* reported some of her comments.

Louisa May Alcott, Daniel Shealy (2013). *Little Women: An Annotated Edition*, p.602, Harvard University Press

Coelho, Paulo (2011) *Tears are Words That Need to be Written*, online [Accessed August 2021]

Nin, Anais (1954) *The Diary of Anaïs Nin, Vol. 5* as quoted in *Woman as Writer* (1978) by Jeannette L. Webber and Joan Grumman,

Angelou, Maya (1969). *I Know Why the Caged Bird Sings*, Random House

Brocklesby, E. (2019) *Irongran: How keeping fit taught me that growing older needn't mean slowing down*. Sphere

Chapter 13

Anonymous as quoted in Jasheway, Leigh Anne (2016) *How to Write Better Using Humour*, Writer's Digest Online [Accessed August 2021)

Austen, Jane (1813) *Pride and Prejudice*, T. Egerton

Young, Debbie (2017) *Murder in the Manger*, Hawkesbury Press

Chapter 14

De Groot, Jerome (2009) *The Historical Novel*, Routledge

Chapter 16

Burns, Robert, (1794) Red, Red Rose, Burns Poetry Foundation Online [Accessed August 2021]

Chapter 19
Jones, Wendy H. (2019) *Motivation Matters*, Scott and Lawson
Frankopan, Peter (2016) *The Silk Roads: A New History of the World*, Bloomsbury Paperbacks
Rutherford, Edward (2021) *China*, Hodder & Stoughton

ACKNOWLEDGMENTS

Grateful thanks go to all the authors who contributed to this book, sharing their expertise and passion so freely. Without them this book would not be possible.

Thank you to all those who have been so incredibly supportive of this project and have encouraged me to keep going. My first foray into the world of publishing other authors was much less frightening because of you.

ABOUT THE AUTHOR

Wendy H Jones is the award-winning, international best-selling author of the *DI Shona McKenzie Mysteries*. Her Young Adult Mystery, *The Dagger's Curse* was a finalist in the Woman Alive Readers' Choice Award. She is also The President of the Scottish Association of Writers, an international public speaker, and runs conferences and workshops on writing, motivation and marketing worldwide. Her first children's book, *Bertie the Buffalo*, was released in December 2018 with *Bertie Goes to the Worldwide Games* following in May, 2021, *Motivation Matters: Revolutionise Your Writing One Creative Step at a Time and Marketing Matters: Sell More Books* are the first book in the Writing Matters series. The third book in the *Fergus and Flora Mysteries* will be published in 2021. Her new author membership *Authorpreneur Accelerator Academy* launched in January 2021. She also produces *The Writing and marketing Show* weekly podcast

She lives in Scotland where her books are based. She loves reading, travelling, and meeting new people, preferably all at once and is spreading her wings in this direction once more. Wendy also loves helping others to follow their writing dreams. She believes writing is the best job in the world.

ALSO BY WENDY H. JONES

DI Shona McKenzie Mysteries

Killer's Countdown

Killer's Craft

Killer's Cross

Killer's Cut

Killer's Crew

Killer's Crypt

Cass Claymore Investigates

Antiques and Alibis

Writing Matters

Motivation Matters

Marketing Matters

Bertie The Buffalo

Bertie the Buffalo

Bertie Goes to the Worldwide Games

Bertie the Buffalo Colouring Book

Bertie Soft Toy

Lightning Source UK Ltd.
Milton Keynes UK
UKHW022017260821
389499UK00011B/220